D0436035

ALSO BY BRENDA HILLMAN

POETRY

White Dress

Fortress

Death Tractates

Bright Existence

Loose Sugar

Cascadia

Pieces of Air in the Epic

Practical Water

CHAPBOOKS

Coffee, 3 A.M.

Autumn Sojourn

The Firecage

AS EDITOR

The Poems of Emily Dickinson

*The Grand Permission: New Writings
on Poetics and Motherhood*
[WITH PATRICIA DIENSTFREY]

*Writing the Silences: Selected Poems
of Richard O. Moore*
[WITH PAUL EBENKAMP]

SEASONAL WORKS WITH LETTERS ON FIRE

WESLEYAN UNIVERSITY PRESS

SEASONAL

WORKS

BRENDA

WITH

HILLMAN

LETTERS

ON

FIRE

MIDDLETOWN, CONNECTICUT

WESLEYAN POETRY

Published by Wesleyan University Press
Middletown, CT 06459

Library of Congress Control Number: 2013939069
Library of Congress Cataloging-in-Publication Data
is available upon request

Design and composition by Quemadura
Printed on acid-free, recycled paper
in the United States of America

Wesleyan University Press is a member
of the Green Press Initiative. The paper
used in this book meets their minimum
requirement for recycled stock.

NATIONAL
ENDOWMENT
FOR THE ARTS
A great nation
deserves great art.

This project is supported in part by an award
from the National Endowment for the Arts.

TO VANISHED & VANISHING SPECIES
TO JOHN KEATS & WILLIAM BLAKE
TO THE AVOCET & THE ANT
TO OUR PARENTS IN LATE AGE
TO THE CANDLE & THE BURNT MATCH
TO ROBERT DUNCAN & BARBARA GUEST
TO SCIENCE & THE ANCESTORS
TO OUR BROTHERS BRENT & BRAD
TO NATURE & THE WORD NATURE
TO GARY SNYDER & FORREST GANDER
TO THE OUTLAW & THE ELECTRON
TO PINES ON SIERRA GRANITE
TO INVERNESS & OUR CHILDREN, TO COLE & ELLA
TO JOSEPHINE, HAZEL, FIONA & FINN
TO OULIPO & OCCUPY, TO THE BATEAU
TO C. D. WRIGHT & LYN HEJINIAN
TO BOOKSTORES, TO KLM & CC
TO THE GROUP READING PROUST IN THE GARDEN
TO BAUDELAIRE, MICHAEL O & MICHAEL P
TO PARIS, TO NORMA COLE & WALTER BENJAMIN
TO POETS IN NORWAY, BERLIN & CHINA
TO POETS IN LIBYA, MYANMAR, SEOUL & BRAZIL
TO THE SPIRITS AWAKE IN THE NIGHT, TO BODIES
TO WOMEN AWAKE IN THE WORLD
TO PEOPLE MOANING AT GAS PUMPS, TO THE STUDENTS
TO PROTESTING CORPORATE VIOLENCE
TO DUST IN FORECLOSED HOUSES, TO FACTS
TO MARIE HOWE & BRADLEY MANNING
TO HUMANS AT SAINT MARY'S, TO THE SQUIRRELS
TO PROSE, TO LINDA S & JANE V
TO CAL BEDIENT, 'ANNAH SOBELMAN & THE CATS
TO FOOD & THE FUTURE OF POETRY
TO CHILDREN LEARNING TO SPELL, TO THE SPELL
TO FRAN LERNER & NAN NORENE
TO HUMAN & NONHUMAN MEANING, TO LICHEN
TO LEON LEARNING TO READ
TO THE WARBLERS OF CALIFORNIA, TO BASEBALL
TO BOB UPSTAIRS WORKING
TO LOVE & THE UNSAYABLE
TO THE FIRE IN EVERYTHING

CONTENTS

I . ON THE MIRACLE OF NAMELESS FEELING

To Spirits of Fire After Harvest · 3

Some Kinds of Reading in Childhood · 4

The Fuel of an Infinite Life · 5

Grammar of This Life at Noon · 6

Geminid Showers & Health Care Reform · · · · · · · · · · · · · · · · · · · 7

Late Autumn Storms at Pigeon Point · 8

At the Solstice, a Yellow Fragment · 9

Early Sixties Christmas in the West · 10

The Vowels Pass By in English · 11

Something Has Been Reading the Fireroots · · · · · · · · · · · · · · · · 12

The Body Politic Loses Her Hair · 13

In High Desert Under the Drones · 14

Between Semesters, the Fragments Follow Us · · · · · · · · · · · · · · · · 15

We Saw the Ǝ Look Back · 16

I Heard Flame-Folder Spring Bring Red · · · · · · · · · · · · · · · · · · · 17

En Route to Bolinas, a Rose · 18

In the Room of Glass Breasts · 19

Equinox Ritual with Ravens & Pines · 20

To Leon, Born Before a Marathon · 21

Fable of Work in the World · 22

A Halting Probability, on a Train · 23

In Summer, Everything Is Something's Twin · · · · · · · · · · · · · · · · · 24

To Stem the Time We Spent · 25

Facelessbook · 26

Two Summer Aubades, After John Clare · 27

The Practice of Talking to Plants · 28

Ecopoetics Minifesto: A Draft for Angie · · · · · · · · · · · · · · · · · · · 29

Foggy Animist Morning in the Vineyard · 30

Previous Dawn in the Next Field · 31

West Marin Night During Perseid Showers · · · · · · · · · · · · · · · · · 32

For One Whose Love Has Gone · 33

Patience Swoons in the Sword Ferns · 34

Between the Fire & the Flood · 35

Between the Souls & the Meteors · 36

Moaning Action at the Gas Pump · 37

Elegy for an Activist in Winter · 38

Autumn Ritual with Hate Turned Sideways · · · · · · · · · · · · · · · · · 39

Rituals with Food Before the Feast · 40

After the Feast at Year's End · 41

Report on Visiting the District Office · 42

After a Death in Early Spring · 43

Imperishable Longing to Be with Others · · · · · · · · · · · · · · · · · · · 44

The Hour Until We See You · 45

Till It Finishes What It Does · 46

After a Very Long Difficult Day · 47

A Spiral Tries to Feel Again · 48

You Were in Sunlight Being Prepared · 49

On the Miracle of Nameless Feeling · 50

II. A SENSE OF THE LIVELY UNIT

As the Roots Prepare for Literature · 53

Summer Mountain Lightning & Some Music · · · · · · · · · · · · · · · · 54

The Elements Are Mixed in Childhood · 55

At the Snow Line in Summer · 56

Sky of Omens, Floor of Fragments · 57

The Seeds Talk Back to Monsanto · 58

Coda: Suggested Activism for Endangered Seeds · · · · · · · · · · · · · · · 59

The Nets Between Solstice & Equinox · 60

Very Far Back in This Life · 61

To the Writing Students at Orientation · 62

The Letters Learn to Breathe Twice · 63

Local Warming & Early Autumn Butterflies · · · · · · · · · · · · · · · · · 64

Halfway Through Civilization, Late to Another · · · · · · · · · · · · · · · 65

Imitating a Squirrel at my Job · 66

Experiments with Poetry Are Taken Outdoors · · · · · · · · · · · · · · · · 67

A Short Walk During Late Capitalism · 68

A Quiet Afternoon at the Office · 74

A Quiet Afternoon at the Office II · 75

When the Occupations Have Just Begun · · · · · · · · · · · · · · · · · · · 76

After the Orionids, Near the Plaza · 77

From the Dictionary of Indo-European Roots · · · · · · · · · · · · · · · · 78

Short Anthem for the General Strike · 79

Mists From People As They Pass · 80

Types of Fire at the Strike · 81

o—o—o o—o—o o—o—o o—o—o · 82

A Brutal Encounter Recollected in Tranquility · · · · · · · · · · · · · · · 83

& the Tents Went Back Up · 85

2 Journal Entries During Occupy SF · 86

An Almanac of Coastal Winter Creatures · · · · · · · · · · · · · · · · · · · 87

The Second Half of the Survey · 88

Lyrid Meteor Showers During Your Dissertation · · · · · · · · · · · · · · 89

Poem of Hope, Almost at Equinox · 90

Radical Lads, Blisters & Glad Summers · 91

Mystical Lichen Falls Through the Fonts · 92

Smart Galaxies Work with Our Mother · 93

In the Evening of the Search · 105

ACKNOWLEDGMENTS & NOTES · 107

I . ON THE MIRACLE OF NAMELESS FEELING

I went out to the hazel wood
Because a fire was in my head

W. B. YEATS
"The Song of Wandering Aengus"

Hummingbird darted from his perch and stole a spark of fire.
He tucked it under his throat and flew directly back home.
When he arrived at the coast, Coyote was nowhere to be found,
so Hummingbird stashed the fire in the buckeye tree.

JULES EVENS Transcription of
"Where Fire Comes From," a Miwok tale

Hoy que en mis ojos brujos hay candelas.
[Today the candles burn in my witch eyes.]

CÉSAR VALLEJO "Los dados eternos"

Brenda, it doesn't exist. **JACK COLLOM**
Conversational aside, Naropa

ARGUMENT:

microseasons, vowels, panicles, California grasses, existence, sex, the cosmos,
childhood reading, guilt, noons, letters in summer fruit, autumn equinox,
the stalk market, stemming the crisis, termites, winter electricity, the six-
ties, learning the y, solstice, spirits, wars we hate, motives, Candlemas, mar-
gins, spring songs, people with birthdays in May, Tesla, memory loss, deserts,
Claudia & Don in the desert, summers in the Sierra, crosses in vineyards, the
nineties, parents' old age, codex, loops in consonants, drones, the body's nerves,
spoken bird poetry, candles in the witches' eyes—these, my love, are made of
fire—

Between earth
& its noun, i felt a fire . . .

—What does it mean by "i," Mrs?
—It means, (& i quote): one
    of the vowels in the brain
        & some of the you's—;

we were interested in the type of thing
humans can't know,
interested in kinds of think animals think
—a rabbit or a skink! (*Eumeces skiltonianus*)
        when autumn brings a grammar,
    wasps circle the dry stalks
    & you can totally
    see through amber ankles dangling
        in dazzle under our lord the sun
        of literature—

Between noon & its noun,
there were ridged
& golden runes on pumpkins . . . bluish
            gourds—in the fields . . .
        (their white eyes lined up
            inside)—Wait a sec. Please
don't nail the door shut. The air is friendly
& non-existent as Veronica's veil— . . .

Earth, don't torment your fool,
your ambassador clown. Bring
the x of oxygen & sex, a fox
running sideways, through present noon—

Do you remember Picture Day?
   Then, when the packets came back—
in each child's eyes:
      incomprehensible fire—;
  you were ordinary,
in the sense of: the endangered west;—
your mother wiped the windshield
with a shredded Kleenex
(that's why you deserved your oily treats)—

Inside the school, reading made sparks:
   peril, peril, peril-&-awe;
outside the school, acres of signs
   in cellophane noon, where
under the school, termites take
  the tasty beams into their bodies—
  [*Incisitermes minor*] delicate hairless arms . . .
Save the volcanoes for later,
flame-folder. You did *such* a good job
with the maps!

  The world has created a sickness
but the sickness is being
reversed . . . Consonants
can be reasoned with, but vowels
  start fires—now! breathing
    twice: Now! Here come
the bandit occupiers:
   silence & meaning—

You argue with someone at work. The chemical change
   in your shadow meets the dry grass at the edge
   of his shadow like an adolescent planning on
   burning a field, or the love you wanted
   to have later with another, the memory of what
   your energy made before he began to speak.

It is impossible to discuss anything with your boss
   because he has consulted the priest & they
   will never see you again—; you stored that
   in the chamber of geometric symbols, saying
   to the wings above the granary, there is the fact
   of the barren stalks, the pharaoh's dream

of hunger, saying to yourself (a prophetic mute),
   the hour will come someday for fire until
   there are years of storing energy in these postures,
   drawing circles with bones from the nine names
   & lights that make words into sticks for
   winnowing the shadows of falsity or ridicule.

Even the world, wide as it is, cannot exhaust
   the fuel of your life when you are one of
   the interpreters about to escape from the dream
   with your archived & flexible heat, trying
   to keep from hating them at the marketplace,
   to remember what would transform judgment

into action if only you could abandon the gifts as if
   they were nothing, after you & the pharaoh's
   huts are long gone; the dream will not be
   idle when it touches the tip of the match
   to the willing field after the harvest—

FOR BBH & SM

The immortals wait in the fields.

& the newt under the laurel (a dragon
      whose three heads argued
   with themselves—),
      the push thistles, *Celastrina echo* butterfly
            with automatic semi-colons
            on its wings—('twill hide
            under the clorox-
   cloud—& that's that! some punctuation
is just too sensitive to
be outside—)
            Stubby white
   teeth on that baby vole:
      smile on its face—screeep!   like
      gnostic Jesus, its comma-comma-comma
      claws. Clause—verbless mosquito-egg
         daylight . . .
                  Worker, dreamer:
your soul has slept with
            countesses so long
      his hands still smell like money!
            He says to himself:
      my lord the sun has thrown
   his sexual shadow upon me . . .   (oops!

Where did it go?)
—It's just fallen behind something.
(What has?)
—Whatever you lost.

Behind the galaxy, there was a flute:
sound was making love to sound;
time was making sound
          to sexual, textual, lexical space—
  we worked too hard, we lay
near fields from which they gathered plastics—
    mimics & contortionists—under the ping-ping
of meteors, under made-up constellations;

the planet flew through space junk
while the Health Care Bill was being penned
  with pens from Chantix, pens from Lidoderm
    & Protinix, with pens
  from Actos, Lamosil, & Celebrex;

late autumn made a fire in us;
    the cosmos waited for a sign;
the soul was waiting for the mind,
fat chickadees waited for sweet fennel
    [*Foeniculum vulgare*] & nameless
        asters on side streets where drones
           take violins to the Queen—
       what kind of drones?
          The sounds fly out, for thee—
we slept as many as the anyway
  where meaning met material, that is,
inside the personal,
    that is, for love of earth—

LATE AUTUMN STORMS AT PIGEON POINT

after Richard O. Moore

Existence tells the lighthouse
I am your pigeon, then *crash!*
we didn't know
it had a window!
Autumn asks its summer:
what if we are only sound
tracking itself, flare
of a fishing boat
(the sea shines purple in);
the body casts its shadow
down the coast,
noon onto the mezzanine—
edge of a thought, a main
but not the only thing. You struggle
to endure your life,
a screen of symbols made of fire;
a nothing calls its something,
its stray hope, no gain;
anarchic music climbs
the tower to turn
the key inside to sing—

Our lord of literature
   visits my love,
they have gone below,
they have lost their way
among the tablets
of the dead—;

     preeeee—dark energy—woodrat
  in the pine, furred thing
     & the fine,
a suffering among syllables, stops
  winter drops from cold,   cold,
miracle night   (a fox
     deep in its hole under yellow
    thumbs of the chanterelles,
    (no: gold. Gold thumbs, Goldman Sachs
     pays no tax . . . (baby goats
in the pen, not blaming God,
    not blaming them—

(alias: buried egg of the shallow-helmet turtle
    [*Actinemys marmorata*]
alias: thanks for calling the White House
     comment line))))

For your life had stamina
from a childhood among priests
& far in the night,
beyond the human realm, a cry
released the density of nature—

It takes all the strength of the girl & her mother holding the knife to slice the holiday bird. Lipton Onion Soup flakes floating in the pan. One pinch of irreverent parsley recalls a belief in plants having feelings. The father reads Camus by the fire. Each book is a Bethlehem. The crèche has an arch where violence is delayed.

> Around the teenage galaxy
> a halo of dark matter
>
> In the nearby desert   iron & silicon
>
>   Between the dimensions
> in a disciplined curved sleep
> fat cherubs assert their right to exist
> for they make more sense
>   than McNamara about Communists

Patterns float independently on the girl's apron. Mr. Postman by the Marvelettes. Like Demeter, the mother is great at using leftovers, & the daughter finds a skill for bringing fragments from the dead: *My. heart. aches. &. a. drowsy. numbness.* The brothers play chess: thump-thump, wooden-skirted figures on ovals of green felt.

—& the owl drops flowers
from its eyes [*Dentaria californica*]—
the raceme, the stubbed stem lands straight
in the woods—as the ancients do;
on a hazel branch, a cocoon
  hoists itself ... with a worm's mind—;

i-eee is released in winter
  as humans hold bones to the fire—
they were there a long time,
      (interpreting the dead loves
as meaning seeped through the cracks
  of centuries held by everyone—);

  the ocean rises by inches—when
the wave withdraws, plovers pick evidence
  from married footprints as the lyric does,
      or sanity ... Luminescent creatures
    sink red in the sand—
for they have swallowed ... all 3 sunsets!

& the vowels pass by in English,
  the ruined banisters of the A, a bridle-
ring of the O, the saddle of the U
    brought from the underworld;
i had to negotiate with devils
  to retrieve even this much
from the language of the colonizers—

—*aw aw*: crows' eyebrows . . .
The termites have hastily married—soon
they'll drop *veined* wings—till their vows
are outside! In the woods,
a shaman moment . . . tries a cure:
pleiades of sun,   a thrush [*Catharus guttatus*]
brings spots to you, a seedful anarchist—

The magicks are merging.
Lambs swell in the bellies of the ewes;
the great dead approach,
famished for winter berries . . .
What is the enigma
you carry halfway to equinox,
your soul feeling his own princely skin
in the back seat?

Origins of expression—in the caves,
the fury of nations,
the handmade stars of lovers' cries,
the abstract stroke—; stop telling us
what to do, Indo-European languages!
everything has been eating the fireroots,
its fluffy hatchlings scratch along—
it says to itself:
we are on loan from a seamless realm
—in the pledge, dot-dot,
—in the syllable of the clause
(You're just making that up)
Am not. (Are too.)
Am not.

THE BODY POLITIC LOSES HER HAIR

(A HAIBUN)

Words started to fall out of sentences in earnest around the time of the first aerial bombs. They kept falling for most of the 20th century. When i read the word *drone*, my hair falls out in solidarity with old words. Stingless singless honey bees [*Apis mellifera*] or the music drones on & on, but now (at the top of Google), *unmanned*, where the "un" in the "unmanned" looks like little pinchers, the "u" & the "n" like the fingers on a throttle when one of our soldiers bombs a target's wedding while his family members are eating potatoes with tamarind, cardamom, onion,

& the *target's* family falls. The pilot goes home to his dinner. Many are saying look the other way about the drones but my hairs fall out when i look the other way. They absorb zippy displays of colorful internet pain-sperm. The medical industry blames falling hairs on hormone loss alone. They want women to apply a patch of estrogen extracted from penned-up horses. This is the problem with trying to make things simple. Some things get less simple when you think about them, especially if words turn out to be what they used to call an evil twin. Words need air, as Proust noted. You

 can give the word *drone* more air on a sign as Janet is doing here in Nevada while a drone flies over. You can burn your fallen hair

when a general indicates that some folks are killed so we can all be free. Actually, he didn't say folks, he said civilians. My hairs are a little too free so they fall. i burn fallen hairs on wedding candles as sacrifice to Sumerian fire deities —burning hair smells like nothing else & on fire it looks like "happy birthday" *salgira at mubarak* سالگـره ات مـبارک ک in Dari: *yoing yoing* greeting the flame in smoky sparky simple sizzle star script ～～～

We are western creatures; we can stand for hours in the sun. We read poetry near an Air Force base. Is poetry pointless? Maybe its points are moving, as in a fire. The enlisted men can't hear. Practice drones fly over-head to photograph our signs; they look like hornets [*Vespula*] with dangly legs dipping in rose circles with life grains. They photograph shadows of the hills where coyotes' eyes have stars. They could make clouds of white writing, cilia, knitting, soul weaving, spine without nerves, dentures of the west, volcano experiments, geometry weather breath & salt. Young airmen entering the base stare from their Hondas; they are *lucky to have a job* in *an economy like this*. The letters of this poem are also lucky to have a job for they are insects & addicts & thieves. Volcanic basalt recalls its rock star father. Creosote & sage, stubby taupe leaves greet the rain. We hold our signs up. We're all doing our jobs. Trucks bring concrete for the landing strip they've just begun.

A cliff   stands out   in winter
Twin ravens drop fire   from its eyes

My inner life is not so inner & maintains the vascular system of a desert plant. I'm grateful to Samuel Beckett & to my high school boyfriend whose drunk father yelled when we closed the door & read *The Unnamable* during the Tet offensive. They prepared me for this. Outside the base we see borax mines in the distance—the colors of flesh, brown, black, peach, pink, bronze. We stand there as the young airmen settle into their routine. The Gnostics noted it is difficult to travel between spheres, you've had to memorize the secret names & the unnamable haunts every aspect of your routine. The names grow heavier as you carry them between the spheres.

BETWEEN SEMESTERS,
THE FRAGMENTS FOLLOW US

As a heron stalks the smart frog,
time stabs the mini-brenda
(we had a winter panic, then it grew—!)
Valved season, approaching Imbolc:
sounds of the newly dead
eee-^^eeyyy, your verbs do little flips
like Russian gymnasts—
thousands of herring purr
through the eelgrass [*Zostara*] with (at the end
of the middle of the end of empire) plastic
buoys, rope, Arabic bronze kelp washed up—
العربية take me too, present tense, take us,
driftwood, each aperture
so mongrel-sized . . .

Across Tomales, children merge with screens,
& farther in: pre-rectangles on the backs
of turtles; there is sexual laughter
in the dune grass—
over the shards, stars buckle
& wheel . . . Some of the fragments are lost,
Osiris. Your lover will find them
with her quantum style—

from envy's edge,
its middle tooth quite bare till it could sing;
(there!)   (we had tried to distract it)—
It was spring in the park: nests & spears,
puffs in the eucalypts: mitered caps,
    chickadees . . . The Ǝ combed chaos
with its triple prongs, some of its
                        moves, unfit for sanity;
until it lived another sense without
our help: pure ᴇɴᴇʀgy:

    wᴇll, that caused quitᴇ a shamblᴇs!
it livᴇd its lifᴇ, ᴇɴchantᴇdly

FOR ER

to the jack-knifed tulip—
smart shy underachieving red,
     its idle set too low . . . Week of quinces
leaning into plum. Teaching *The Aeneid*
for the twelfth time. Is Virgil anti-war? One
student notes "Virgil really cares"
   what the weapons are made of: Turnus
aims his spear of ilex & burning hemp—
  Geese sound like puppies overhead,
  the leader barking in the skinny rain—

Ceaseless Empire Trojan Roman
Ottoman British U.S.A., treating tribal lands
like layers on a big old onion. Hard to be cheerful
  at work. Fuck cheerful. Women
in Kandahar make $2 a month; our people
tweet & sleep through the wars,
  our soggy purses lie open, the eyes
  of the dollar bills stare up from the floor—

Mother, send your owl to the West
 for the soul has hung
  the great hurt on a branch
& the omens will take it away.
   One of its wings hangs down
a little bit, its markings fitly imagined,
its feathers all prayed about—

EN ROUTE TO BOLINAS, A ROSE

twisting on the gate—
not *eglantine*—should we say "teen" or "tyne"?
Keats is our valentine & the cat
that bears his name—
just past the bridge, the soul
flies through when juncos pass
like action in a Coen Brothers film,
short grasses grow crisp & cry out,
we are so close to chaos then;

the guests lingered
by the red door, murmuring goodbyes
after a gentle lunch, your mother's spirit
looked down from the hill, coyote
—waiting—near the hen,
a shaman with a pollen glance.
Hop over the stream in your boots
& say, No need to lift
the salmon from the stream this year;
the waters are full—

FOR AM

Around each word we're hearing,
there spins an original flame;
    the unborn wait in a circle of commas,
 upright robins wheel to Wheeler
& termites with arms in their heads
      dig under the chairs—-

It is impossible to describe the world;
that's why you get sleepy listening to poetry.
    The writer skates but spring takes
the gold (*ooo don't let her fall in sequins*). Dusk
      buzzes in its meaning kit.
  Maybe we drank too much but that's not it;
her sexy voice enchanted everyone. You were
  drawn to poetry by something nothing
satisfies but poetry: boundless sensation,
an abstract tone—then one day, two simple words
    could made you weep: *Unreal . . . City . . .* Not
mostly; mostly they didn't make you weep. But still.
    Unreal . . . (then that big pause:) . . .
City. . . . Look at that smart
  italic guy over there waiting to be in a stanza:
      Sat low our lord of literature
      for he was very tired—

Outside the room, the spell ends,
the vowel of an owl/the owl of a vowel
  dives onto a warm body, the ruined gardens
    of the State, tended by the great dead—
You were called by a silence you can't understand.
You're grown up now. You can read all night
    if you want, in the bride's bed—

FOR CA & CL

—so we said to the somewhat: Be born—
    & the shadow kept arriving in segments,
   cold currents pushed minerals
up from the sea floor, up through
coral & labels of Diet Coke blame shame
     bottles down there—
    it is so much work to appear!

unreadable zeroes drop lamps
    as mustard fields [*Brassica rapa*]
gold without hinges, a vital
     echo of caring . . . On the census,
just write: *it exists!* Blue Wednesday
     bells strike the air like forks
   on a thrift store plate,
& the shadow moves off to the side . . .

In the woods, loved ones tramp through
   the high grass; they wait in a circle
     for the fire to begin;
they throw paper dreams & sins upon
       the pyre & kiss, stoking the first
   hesitant flame after touching a match
to the bad news—branches are thrust back
across myths before the flame catches—;
ravens lurch through double-knuckled
    pines & the oaks & the otherwise;
a snake slithers over serpentine
then down to the first
    dark where every cry has size—

FOR EK & MS

When you were born,
they fell in love with sleep;
doves delivered the five wax notes;
a pointed moon brought in its radiance.
Some were strapping distance on their feet
as you cried out among the architectures;
month of the fiddlehead,
hounds-tongue, coltsfoot;
month of the normal rains—

& though earth is somewhat tired
of the new, there would never
not be news again. Tall wild stalks
circled the lake,
stirring shouting into the street,
a little gray trash scattered;
& when the runners finally passed,
rebel seeds had joined an auxiliary
race. You brought
two kinds of hours
into days; one kind was blank;
one had your expression on its face—

You threw your book in the ocean,
    a big wave hooked it
down through meaning,
up through noon;
      —why did you do that, sister?
      —chaos enchanted me, mister
        A plover stole the cover
        on a breezelet from the sea.

It's wild to give up your labor—;
wind shook the water like paper:
    half a fable, half an april
in a kingdom by the sea.
        —You stole that from Poe.
        —Did not.
        —Did too.
A big fish took it,
a halibut with a habitat—
    down to molting sea lions
& serpentine grains below.

It's hard to give up your labor
    but you never owned it, did you,
    nor did the volcano, the glad,
the flat, the red, sad miracle;
it burned between you & the reader
    who heard with an oval mind
      a reedy local music
      in a curved time.

FOR GWF

What is a self when riding along
  clakkety-clack, in the rain—?
(*Grieving intensity, it is a fire egg . . .*
  A wishbone cave in a book on the history of flame)

  —& the thought went on without you,
    as you slept with the book in your lap
  as the book slid down
  to the moving floor,
  as the *A* set one foot down
in the train of your thought . . .

If the track were missing a *tie*
  there would be a danger,
but the tie (once called a "sleeper")
      has been put back—

& the passengers who sleep nearby—
    the unraveling of relation
      while the train moves past
    the calm towns, the nights, the crows—
  are a self. Sort of. Others
arrive in love & blue math, to help you out—

Tell your mother's first syllable the moth
    to bring its trigon to the doorframe . . .
the universe is speeding up,
electrons swallowed by the rose—
     you work so hard, too-hard-too-hard.
Humans have made a disaster but
     —but what, sister?
     —but nothing, pencil. tttap-tap.
Such a short season between dogwood
& tiger-lily. Sunscreen sinks
between hairs on your arm. Western yew
   [*Taxus brevifolia*] requests a canopy . . .

     People come here for their bit of joy,
they gather in western towns,
   radicals growing weed in the woods, makers
     of quilts & clouds, loggers, keepers
of the sick with their hounds; they
   rest on weekends, in bars,
     for love without reason or ledger;
   Castor & Pollux sink in the cougar's cry . . .
   in a month or so, the sky will swallow Gemini—

   Hurry now, for the hive is ill,
the cedar branch bows low as the wagon passes
& earth lies in the long earth bed . . .
   Plenty of accidents come your way
   but today you are otherwise,
today you train yourself to be safe, to work
   as Billy has trained the little horse—

FOR CH

TO STEM THE TIME WE SPENT

—their being time at present—blue:) LESLIE SCALAPINO

The ancestors don't crowd us.
They become a kind wind
to let us pass through. Stems
      of avena... stripe-stripe, behind
their mother, stripestripestripe, baby skunks
have entered the spicy ground like a ribbon
    falling from a girl who's learning to read.

 Harbor seals are molting now. A few.
A woman stays visible in stems of her words—
 Stems from the Triassic ooze from
disaster & now
      nothing can stem the crisis
       (from *stemma*, to stammer. Stand
& stammer...) Oyster,
embrace your inner Halliburton.

From a hill, in a dream of time *I i* i i
   brought some extra kindling to the fire...
like i in every font,
  we intend to make some changes;
we hope to learn to breathe before we die.
The grain spirits have abandoned
   the painting & spread
  wild flax to the field. ield. iel. e.
Please don't rise before i rise;
      acetylcholine brings its arrows
to the spine & causes my arms to move.

My country's addicted to Facelessbook, it friends them then bombs them or sometimes it bombs then friends. The drones are faceless when they fly over mountains friending the villagers & the queen bee they would friend if they could find her body would also be faceless.

huckleberry oak armor-plated wasp gall

an eyeless drone   chews   its way out

Some tell me to relax, it's a stage in late capitalism, just accept this till the revolution then get guns. Dadaists suggested blind interventions with screaming & staying drunk. Facelessbook makes it complicated when people are nice. After our loved one died, we put the crematorium on the credit card. i told the two young Activation Representatives at Metro PCS—they were very sweet, probably someplace in the Midwest—it's not just that his phone was lost, he had died, he would not be using the phone, & they asked, Did i remember what kind? was it one of the kinds with the flap? It took first Brandy & then Steve an hour to retrieve the security code. Please let's stop calling it "his" code, stop using "his" now—& then i thought, no, the dead should keep their pronouns. Keep geometry, especially roundness. i tried contacting him in a trance; his person hadn't stopped leaking specifics. i couldn't tell if he was happy but he said, "Man, the food here is great."

lady in a narrow skirt

A tent   of sky
the stars   are Braille

*1. towhee [*Pipilo crissalis*] wakes a human*

pp   cp cp cp chp chp

PPPPPPPPPPPP
cppppcpp cpp   cpp

(a woman tosses)
    Gulf disaster   ster sister
      aster aster as asp
ppp cp cp p   bp bp BP BP
  scree sreeeeem we

we we didn't
neee neeed to move so fast

2. woman in red sweater to hummingbird

    sssssss we sssssss weee
no i'm not not   sweeet not
sweeeeetie i'm not
    something to eeeeeat

FOR JS

Mama & i, we talk to plants, for
we are short girls close to the ground
    & speech is the golden miracle—;
i learn to write while she says *honey* (making a fire-pouch
in the *y*) to a speckled
    banana whose existence is energy broth.
To limp chrysanthemums she says *Come on* & drops
a Bayer aspirin in; i curve our letters near a *cholla*
    after it lent some needles to my leg—

We're not good relaxers, childhood & i,
we suffer a leafy need while God is a missing
    hypotenuse. We'll not a dreaded dandelion meet
    before her voice arrives at low violets.
In summer, when spicy seeds escape so fine
a pepper tree to make sashay for the *lahn-ger-ay* drawer,
    we speak to spices they put on Jesus,
    those poor bright spices staring in the dark . . .
He hath numbered every hair on your head, she said,
    meaning she hath numbered the hairs . . .

    when we are out with our strangeness
in the west—she in her desert, i on a mountain
crouching near *Lilium parvium*
with the same amount of frail our mother feels,
    —it will be quiet for a while but syllables
are there: inside a leaf, a syllable,
        inside a syllable, a door—

A—At times a poem might enact qualities brought from Romantic poetry, through Baudelaire, to modernism & beyond—freedom of form, expressivity, & content—taking these to a radical intensity, with uncertainty, complexity, contradiction;

B—such a poem employs knowledge from diverse disciplines—including scientific vocabularies, but it does not privilege only the human. Research includes rural & urban wilds as well as knowledge from all cultures; creative forms bring together earth & spirit, rejecting no sources, including the personal;

C—its energies shuttle across binaries: realism/non-realism, rationality/irrationality, refuting received authority;

D—such a poem like an animal could graze or hunt in its time, exploring each word, carrying symbolic rhythms, syntax & images directly between the dream & the myth; the imagination does not reject the spirit world;

E—then a poem is its own action, performing practical miracles:
   1. "the miracle of language roots"—to return with lexical adventures
   2. "the miracle of perception"—to honor the senses
   3. "the miracle of nameless feeling"—to reflect the weight of the subjective, the contours of emotion
   4. "the miracle of the social world"—to enter into collective bargaining with the political & the social

F—& though powerless to halt the destruction of bioregions, the poem can be brought away from the computer. The poet can accompany acts of resistance so the planet won't die of the human.

FOGGY ANIMIST MORNING IN THE VINEYARD

. . . this is not me; this is portable me. JULIAN ASSANGE

—**t t t t t t**he letters
are lonely, they wait under the vines,
their crucifix groups spread out
from the eye . . . the grapes drop down
from stem to node where roots
meet the fleabane seed &
fox meets the vole;—

shadows wait under the stakes
as anarchy waits in the novel or sex
waits in college, a feeling
individual letters have before
a word is spelled—;
middle of summer:
t t t t ermites riddle   the wood
near houses   with coded gates;
the workers have been bused in
at dawn. A man bends down to check
a meter in the field, or,
is that a heron—
tHHHHe
rows brighten in the sun as
meaning presses to the back
of the page, the space
you make/unmake to eat, fly
up, drop wings at some point, brain-
light termite. Poet.

   —goodness! your pockets
loaded with fallen plums,
  you walk like a pregnant grandmother—
a rabbit runs under the vine, its ears
like the *lls* in *Hillman*.
  Earth spirits stand by; they've come
from the classics;
    a spiral of nothing is pierced
by its own axis

        the sky spins around
a field of chicory [*Cichorium intybus*],
shadows silverado some sticks
   in the road,
\\\\//// |||| as if a spoiled emperor
 had thrown his bed to the amphitheatre . . .

In the hills, workers & owners
   wake with opposite terrors;
  tiny flies skim the grout in short
 white houses. Each moment
is a crowd. Why so angry?
   Your enemy was anxious
& has moved away; she's forgotten
 even the hem of your dress.
At least, can you drive less? At least
 don't eat at the Bar-B-Q—

The sugars drop down in the berries,
   no longer specific. That mangy deer
sleeps the summer off.   You've been here
the night away, a body with its bit
   of local pain. Under the hazel: spots
on satyr anglewings [*Polygonia satyrus*] spaced
   unevenly. Spikenard bundles
poof up from huge stalks.
  ["Then took Mary a pound of
ointment of spikenard, very costly, & anointed
the feet of Jesus . . ."]
   Friday self-dislike is replaced
  by earlier mild energy—

   Fiery rocks hurl themselves through
"heavenly dust"—(Why are 'e' & 'r' reversed
in *fiery* while *f* stays on first—)
You've been up the night away, a silhouette
of clauses: claws in the dust
making you sneeze. Vast a thought,
  vast a sky waiting for morning fog.

   Pour down, light strands of the difficult;
   the moon will not rise
   with its golden axe of being—
If the fog is too thick, the meteors are on line:
http://topaz.streamguys.tv/~spaceweather/index.html
  The first void is God waiting; that
continues, of course. Then a couple of pings.
  It sounds like the back of the universe
  is getting acupuncture::
@@** a spinning is entered by needles
  of gloved rain—

FOR JS

FOR ONE WHOSE LOVE HAS GONE

There was a crack
in ecstasy; it split the oak
with flameless fire.
A raptor left good bones
in the divided tree (the spine?
of a mouse?) & then flew off
for a muffled sanctuary . . .

Some say *get*
over it, but there you are,
surrounding it. Slant sun
shines in. Bring it along,
bone-reader, bring the banquet.

FOR CN

Deep in the earth a grief had been heard.
Right behind that, a local mystery.
—What do you mean by mystery, Mrs?
—The parallel series that sink in the mist.
Tentacles of limestone: Jupiter
           drops through Pegasus
    & huckleberries line up
    like eyes in the matinee.

Deep in the earth,
an unprecedented seed.
Hearing leans from the words—
early, earth, hearth all have ears in them.
    i can hardly bear it yet i go out.
—What can't you bear? (which
      by the way also has an ear in it.)
    The tender exactingness. Electrons
swoon in the sword fern,
Polystichum munitum, & after the rain,
sexy tips of celadon; sori breathe
    under the fronds.
—Womanly shadow, why don't you try?
—*Can'tcan'tcan'tcan't.* My love & i
    are tired, & cannot fly . . .

—OK then; it is noon in the orange
you wish for; it is night
 in the wretched war. A gasp
    in all creation— a stem
    pushes up, through its prime—

The soil breaks apart in its lost fame,
     far from the Pliocene now.
A caul of fog from Mt. Diablo
down to my first husband's grave.
Not much grows between granite
& serpentine; the glassy edges gasp.
     Sound, you have eaten the lyric.
     Soil, you're the crushed
         thoughts of stars—

Years of not getting enough sleep;
awake at 5 to worry about the planet.
     (*Now i am sound.*
      Now i have eaten the lyric.)
     We think of adulthood
as layers of panic, *is it, is it, is it,*
     in the deodar cedar, the squirrel
makes nano-chatter to the jay—

 When as a child we made dirt soup,
my brother stirred the gravel with a stick.
     Summer barbecues had ended;
someone scraped the metal
     on the grill (*it it it it*).
The desert was calm; i get calm
    just thinking about it. Now a warm
    storm coming in. Creek brain
puts bells on, i talk to the ground, then
     i push an acorn in the grave.
Something nothing something nothing
(*it it it it*) something saves all of it—

The ancestors turn in the sycamore,
leaves like hunched-over squirrels.
A freeze might take the lemon tree.
   That thing of dozing "over a book,"
the writer just godpowder now.
Miles up, sparks dragged through
      meteors; miles down,
creatures eat rock mixed with fire—

Someone prays for you
even if you don't like it. Our suicides
   sleep in the mind of a word.
   We want our mother
not to have suffered. Moonbeams
 snake where the tanoak shivers.
   We want our father
not to have suffered, or the three cats,
sprinkled with western dawn—

     The little baby sleeps on his side,
his dream face turned to the woods;
   a fox sleeps with its mouth of color;
& the O in your head, the damaged vowel,
where the skin rises to meet the wound,
   what does that spell?
   —i don't know, i don't know
(since it got to go on living) but
seems like basically it's kind of
   a combination: everything
means everything plus
   there is no hidden meaning—

MOANING ACTION AT THE GAS PUMP

*. . . in the tragic world, all moaning tends to
consider itself music.* NICOLE LORAUX

Soon it will be necessary to start a behavior of moaning outdoors when
pumping gas . . . That capital *S* is a sort of gas nozzle. Pulling up, beginning
a low moaning action, pulling a deep choral moan with cracks up through the
body, the crude through the cracks of sea & earth, pulling neurotransmitters
glutamate, acetylcholine, & others across chasms in the nervous system, into
the larynx until the sound acts by itself. So we shred the song to continue.
Meaning morning moaning mourning. i am able to complete 34 moans by
the time i've filled half the tank. City-states outlawed open wailing because it
was not good for democracy, but you will merely be embarrassed even if you
drive a hybrid. Please be embarrassed. Please.

Inside the pump, you can hear a bird, a screech-covered pelican lugged out
of the Gulf with 4 million tons of the used booms in non-leakable plastic, 13
million tons of liquid in nonleakable plastic *5* miles up the road—their *5* has
a leak in it by the way—the moan fans out as you put your head down on the
hood of your car; please moan though the other drivers are staring. Squeak,
there are other animals inside the pump, the great manatee—*Trichechus man-
atus*—you've seen it float like a rug that has something wrapped in it among
grasses that will not return. ***eeeooooiieeoooooouuuuu***, this moan won't be the
same mammal but is a democracy with no false knowledge, the sounds pushed
to the edge of a painting, globs of oil floating to shores of salt-marshes. The
broadcaster says the globs "look like peanut butter," wanting to sound lovable
so we can begin to feel friendly about them. Ever since 3 wars ago the moan
meeting other moans & you ask how to get over it . . . is it like Gilgamesh &
Enkidu, David & Absalom, like Isis & Osiris, like Ishmael & history, is it like
Hecuba & her kids, Cassandra who did not drive, is it like Mary, like
Antigone who could barely lift the body to bury it, probably you don't you
don't have to probably you don't have to get over it—

Only a portion of your life
was captured in your writings; you
            passed through years of bells &
    mists. In warm stone cities parallel
to violence the ones with guns
could never stand for this.
        In a system unchanged by law,
councils, charts of the magistrates, friends
    jailed without notice would never know
what filled the spectrum. Sentences living
            in intimate spaces & a ritual
kindness of strangers saved you;

through the years while cities burned
    without notice, the writings of others
were canceled by violence. Iron bells
            & rifles filled the warm spaces.
Magistrates captured by ritual passed you.
Intimate friends vanished in the councils.
        In a system unchanged by law,
    only you recalled that portion of
the spectrum. The jailed work of
            sentences saved you. In cities
of strangers you infinitely lived, as
now, as always, words are living—

—i pull the hate
on a rope ladder to the resting zone . . .
       H

        H

         H

pull the A on down.

A

 A

 A

     Put that sick A to bed. Get well, A. Pinched
     fire. Bring the T down now
                   T

                     T

                       T

Roman cross before the Christian thing.
Bump bump. Put that T to bed. Put
   that Garamond T
to bed before we kill someone with it. Such as:
 Whack-whack. Weapons contractors in Virginia.
Whack. Get well T. Won't kill with you.
    Now. Being
   able to breathe for the E,
breathe into the prongs. Slide on its back.

            E   E   E
     Put the E to bed. Get well, E.
Weird shapes around campfires
   below the mind.
Tiny fires with hurt earth spirits
   as in Aeschylus. Resting letters now
   so they can live—

When darkness enchants us
in its class of forms & the *about-to-happen*
renders calm, the berries split & snap
in their juices; it's then the dear ginger
cooks on the crown of heat. It's then
the women make a cross in each chestnut;
then the sweet pulp rests in the shells,
after a flight from introverted trees—

Voices curl near the blue flame;
mother & daughter pick moonseeds from
pomegranates, they are taxonomists
& label the peppery fruit . . .
A moment of fear as the meat is carried
with sage, mushrooms & bread—

& the children laugh
though they had been sad;
the baby sleeps in the grown-up bed
near a painting of Mary showing Jesus
to a patron in *des Mittelalters*:
radical energy, frail winter,
styles of realism, Come in—

—the flash, the low cry,
   a storm took the lights—
where were you when the glass broke?
Were you in the field with a startled heart?
   Earth's axis tipped twice in the dark
& nothing gleamed in a singular way—;
      whoodie-whoo went the owl
in the incense bough, & a daffodil
      pushed up too soon
like the thesis in a freshman essay . . .

The dead are patient among the trees,
      visitor greets anti-visitor,
   masked chickadee, masked waxwing
(*masked waxwing* is pretty darn hard to say);
the violent are not carried away,
      they are packaged on Twitter . . .
      & your body is the broker
      for the wound & the miracle
   (though the wound can't wait
to reveal itself & the miracle
      learns the exit in advance—)

Who is poetry for? Truth is, i don't know. The folks at tailgate parties before the game, in their lawn chairs—are they *dying every day for lack of what is found there?*

It's been proposed that we take poems about offshore oil drilling to Congressional staff. My district is shaped like a bouncing blue amoeba. Ironic to drive 20 miles to protest oil drilling in a dreamily-driving-to-the-suburbs depression. Inside the "atrium"—a fountain with ridges—climbing the stairs with Janet & taking the poems like contraband across the threshold. M the district director sits with us; she tells about bills the Congressman will put forth. She is kind & listens carefully while we read to her at a huge table. 3 women, 2 poems.

2 flags hang patiently listening from their poles. i am nervous & want to not sweat & cry in official places, to be calm & believe in the system, as M does. But the system makes us crazy; we've become harpies, harridans, banshees, devils moaning at the gas pump. In *The Oresteia,* underground Furies are paid off by the rational sky gods. Let's be nice now. i want my representative to shriek in Congress, not be polite. Here we are in his office—3 women, 2 poems. i am grateful for their company. We are powerless to save the pelicans &

the manatees. Big oil has bought everything but not my armpits, which are sweating in solidarity with the Commons before the 18th century Enclosure Acts. Sensible limits to use. Oceans could be the Commons. As could volcanoes & the moon. Outside, early spring & light rain. Up the devil mountain, quail & brush rabbits scurry. Janet & i hold our arms out. Calendula deodorant smell mixes with the air & the hurry—

The rains come back, the names,
& herring spawn—far out to sea—
 Cynoglossum blue, here, first—the willow
 opens its catkins to drop
 gold powder near generational nests.

    The humans bury their dear one
in a light wind—the soul
is unafraid. The maker of plots hesitates—
so "out of order": that a son should go first . . .
  Matter flares in the void,
particles of chaos meet particles of song—
thoughts around the edges
of the mind dissolve—

   spirits, spirits, green & brown
   why have you left him here
   even for an hour?
He had a merry laugh & harmed no one.
 Swallows, violet in the violet shadows,
circumfix their ovals. His life
 was magnified by longing.
He loved avenues in cities, Eden,
 the crinkled tops of water;
   he gave up dread for certain
   light on certain clothing—

(PMH 1974–2011)

at the rushing forth   in streets—,
of squares,   where you've been,
  with pewter imports—   star-shaped stones,
shops,   ships stalled in the harbor—;
  [(where they danced
      who had been jailed—)]
      the tyrant   shouting   to his thugs
      firing   on his own—from the wall

In this hour, with your coffee,   specks of cinnamon,
        scarves hung   from architraves,
women   crossing ridged water   of this chaos

  advanced hope,   advanced grief
stones from towers   near burning sand . . .

Once we were with you—
            not to intervene; in that range
      of action, you danced—
who had been jailed—
now ache   at the rushing forth—
      the poet's soul   curved fire
lip of sun where you crouched   under arches;
      how it is now—for you,
      to ask the question

When we part, even for an hour,
you become the standing on the avenue
baffled one, under neon,
   holding that huge
red book about the capital—;

   what will you be in the next hour,
  —bundled to walk
through creamy coins from streetlamps
on sidewalks to your car, past
   candles reflected in windows, while
mineral sirens fade in the don't-
return,—driving home past
   pre-spring plum blossom riot
moments of your thought . . .

     Those trees rush to rust leaves,
each a time-hinge with great energy—
   they can't bear inexactitude.
News of revolts in the squares—there—
  & here, the envious have gone to cafés
to speak in order to leave things out—
   Love, literature is in flames,
it was meant to be specific—;
   you have driven past these rooms
ten thousand times to make your report;
make your report;
   you will never forget how you felt—

Where is the meaning, the old man asked.
The night nurse had put on
his little frowning socks; he lay
on his lifebed, in the dusk, holding
the tail of a comet. Outside
the hospital, creosote;
the cactus wren is such a good packer.
Granite, wild at the hands
of quartz, rose in the saddle
of the mountains (i'm writing this
with a pharmaceutical pen,
at the nexus of science & magic) . . .

When all the visitors
had left the room,
the tiny valve of the pig beat inside
our father's heart, like the spokes
of the sun-disk, in a hieroglyph—
above the squiggly river symbol,
like meaning & its tributaries,
nothingness & art . . . Active one,
the animal is not your emissary.
It is not the decoration you sought;
its beauty runs without your will.
It drives the mystical heart.

You talk to your loved ones
at night. It is a kind of modernism:
color sees into you, thinks a warm
path, a tint of meaning brought
from how you feel. Then, you are double:
the owl calls out, *Tyto alba*,
in your sleep—*scrip scrr*—heart-shaped face
emitting loose nouns . . . Under its turf,
the smart mouse turns; the fierce dead
merge with the recently born
where earlier they emptied what you seek—

How will you be known? Some
registered complaints. You passed them
in the hallway, their new haircuts.
The bosses are known by new wars.
What salmon are left hurry upstream—
cold swaths in the bay. Linnets, by
rose fire at the edges—(*linnet* or *finch*?
the word *edge* has wings made of '*e*');
the moon rests in a mantle
of minutes, its boundaries in back
of the trees. Boundaries
are known by their nothings—;
you will be known by your dreams.

A SPIRAL TRIES TO FEEL AGAIN

The upwelling of the sea continues.
Untold mouths scoop up the tiny krill.
Spin, goes the cog of the snowflake
          on the hill; far inland,
blind litters of the muskrat curl
& in your heart a nameless spiral
          around the blue dot—;

if this were the classics . . .
          but it's not. After the royal
wedding, the kill. Cassandra
is dragged out, the corpse
is dumped into the sea—there!
          fire in the compound—
the spiral tries to free itself
& in the pit, young humans
dance in their murderous awe.

          Not even the seasons,
surely not humans, feel
what the spiral feels,
in the trees, in the trees, the bodies
without organs gasp,
& the sea swells over the evidence.
          Exhausted from the unsayable
the letters pause beside your desk,
in the shadow of sheer flux
     where it's not safe to feel nothing;
outside intention, the words gather—

FOR MD

Sat low our lord
of literature
for he was very tired;
he'd had a fool's time of it—

Rattle-prr, the cricket crrrr,
   click-crick, under the deodar
bad breeze fights frets, repeats
  itself like Theodor;—well,
guess what. There is a season
that does not go
with the wind,
  fights frets & fidgets far—;
you were in sunlight being prepared,
beyond the bridge, the otter pups
  swam blind, at once—we're tired
of the human world. There is
a music that does not go with the fire.
Low grade depression . . .
   In the hills, dark gneiss
in granite, old fire undressed. String
out, fire spirits, underground . . .

Owl swoops down across an oak
still day, *Ramalina menziesii*, lichen
  hangs down. Can't tell which
to prefer: owl or mouse. Sat
low, sat low twice—; there is
  a nature that does not
  go with the mind—

FOR TM

They struggled at sunset
& moonrise, they struggled at sunrise—
then not. It is best to be
the calm one, a diadem. Over
their heads, the galaxies whirled, fires
so hot the sun could not relate;
then, putting all that away . . .

They've brought passion & exhaustion
to the wedding. Lists are finished—
abstraction & realism, details repeated
as in airport carpet. Sometimes passion
will sustain them or an interest in certain
problems. Sometimes in the night
they'll describe the nameless feeling.
Nations praise peace but the miracle
is food—not just for the human,
for the owl, the mouse. & now

they stand as a lighthouse
stands on granite, capped in cloud;
it's unbearable how often
the sun goes down but the next day
is a ship of numbers set on fire.
Their love was nothing, then
was almost everything. The named
& the nameless dream with them there—

FOR SK & MZ

II. A SENSE OF
THE LIVELY UNIT

Forms, flames, and the flakes of flames.
WALLACE STEVENS "Nomad Exquisite"

Burning up myself, I would leave fire behind me.
ROBIN BLASER "The Fire," 1967

If you can't apologize don't eat it
SARAH ROSENTHAL "Sonnet"

*. . . the ocean blew steadily across the long ridges, and from
high-swinging cones, opened by the fiery heat, the winged seeds
drifted downward to the earth.* **GEORGE STEWART** *Fire*

ARGUMENT:

*Forest fires in the west, street protests, for my mother, for my daughter, for
Sharon at Dream Fluff, western streets in spring, "Little J.A. in a Prospect of
Flowers," household hints from the 50s, on removing stains from fabric, protest-
ing drone attacks, mama's handwriting, the clinging of lichen, Diebenkorn
#57, sex between dreams, terminator seeds by Monsanto, bosses selling termi-
nator seeds to peasants, the parents' corrugated tin storage unit in Tucson, spir-
its in the other world, California plants in recipes, to live for love of earth, eat-
ing greens with Jo & G, the beginning of life at the fire vents, intoxicated
protests, students climbing on boxcars, the way letters think, space in mole-
cules, strike, occupy, strike, the sense of the lively unit, without inordinate
grief, on removing stains from galaxies, to mourn & rejoice for the human*

Sound, what is your muse? Just now,
    we found a meaning but too soon—
cckkcckk . . . Dawn sprinklers start &
crickets wheel, they go down-down, dippy
down-down. Smell of toast in the suburbs.
      The West is burning. Our little mother
    prays in her sleep, our father rests
under his new big scar like America.
Ancestors step through flame to get to them.
Beyond air, the galaxies whirl ceaselessly
    as picnic salt—
        Our childhood sight
hath gathered multitudes . . . On streets
    named for forts or saints, news is brought
to foreclosed houses. The medicated grasses wait.
In other deserts, soldiers kill other people's
      parents. Here the unemployed wear boots
  in cafés near terrifying pies
piled high with cream. Wrens make nests
    in cholla. *Cylindropuntia fulgida.* Spirits
stand round in the bodies of doves.

    Do you remember learning to spell?
It's best to bring words slowly into English;
  wrad (the root of *root*) shines
    for centuries underground. It's not
for nothing the shadows are lit when children
are called to literature. Now word
       has gone out that you are here
  as sleepers curve their heat-shapes
to the ground. Hard
  for you to keep steady, i know. The roots
  of your words can see fire, though.

Tesla, maker of homemade lightning, set fire
to his room by mistake. He never
had much of a lover & now they've named
a car for him; & now a tanager in the pine
has perched upright
to put itself in danger for a mate.

If, like a fire, that sound had three sides,
if like a point, a flame, it would be
pure geometry; such objects that strike you
as beautiful, you cannot name.
Tesla moved to the mountains, began
shooting rays, sexual E's the hawk gave back,
into the abstract—days adept
at non-nothingness—far past a life & its shape.

The great resister
stays in you, plodding, then
the blind harpist plays. Between magnetic poles,
they place a motor made of money
to drive the horror of an age—& daily,
these unmanageable patterns, & weekly,
the magnificent ordinary.

The next thing you make will be different.
You stand in the field not yet being
struck, talking to nothing, jagged
& unsure. You knew this
when you started the experiment; you wanted
to be changed & you were—

THE ELEMENTS ARE MIXED IN CHILDHOOD

(AN ESSAY IN RHYME)

Our mother was baptized on a kerosene box, our father was baptized in a creek, & we were baptized in a plaster pool while turquoise ripples played around our feet & desert air poofed up to make the long black robe a nylon buffalo. *It makes your underpants wet*, said our brother. It's strange to be on fire with sins. This is how the past begins: it is the year of the missile crisis; it is the year of Barbie & Ken. Mama studies ridges in her gloves, the congregation sings a hymn while out in the desert, the worm grows tall & nature is a mixed-up miracle.

We strain to see the cross behind our head: not only no penis on Jesus, no Jesus at all. That's how Baptists like it: the invisible is physical. That's the way it is, says Walter Concrete in the news. Talking flames get rid of hell. In college we'll read Emerson; in college we'll meet Robert Duncan dressed like a bat but we don't know that. Go ahead, says curlicue, the mind is what you need to make up & why should a child be dressed like a bat, wings flapping up to her sides like that? Bat-at-at-at.

The congregation sings a hymn, they hold the stanzas up-up-up. Mama studies ridges in her gloves; she is our eternal love. Childhood certainly is odd: everything is everything, earth air beauty fire wood water love blood, time is what you need to mix up & what is anything not god. The choir circles the circles; they're singing to rehearse for glory, fiery stanzas fill our head. That's why words are round in every story; that's why we love music & talk to the dead—

FOR MK

There appeared again
a little thinking cloud—; it was trying
        to figure out how to hover. Just to the right
of the peaks, some fire striations in the granite.
Just to the right of the mind, pines pushed up
from below . . . *scrrrrrip*! A million years pass.
        Letharia volpina drops
from the ponderosa. The gods hold back,
        deprived of terror.
                —*What is it now, Mrs.?*
                —*Not sure what you mean by* now.
                —*You are caught again in the nameless*
                        hour till all of life seems wrapped in it

        That eagle wears its shadow eagle
        on the ground, coasts in the thermals,
barely flaps over the petro-fabric . . .
Bolds, givens. Toxic hours & mute money—
        & lately you hath
                gotten bossy at thy demanding job.
        In summer snow, pinched

nevering bulbs push up like Moscow
churches. Some spikes
        of cold might heal your hurry.
        Effort of vision reversal—but here you are,
still upright at the edge of sound . . .

    & the sound in the field
        was an abstract sound—
      it went nnnn--uuuuuuooo
    (*might have been some mixed-genre insect*
      going on to help nature—)

* * * *

Some of the munitions manufacturers also make prosthetic devices for women vets. Complaints had been filed since 2005 that the arms & legs were sized for men. Now the Pentagon is wising up because, bullet point, 14% of the active forces are females & also, bullet point, 11% are combat forces, which percent is expected to increase in the future, plus half of this population are women of childbearing age. Now there seems to be more attention to making the artificial limbs smaller, but also to making uniform wigs & mastectomy bras. Representatives attend to surveys, cost trends. The V.A. website shows a woman stirring chocolate cake batter with her new arm made of a steel bar with a strap. Here's a graphic of piled-up money from the site:

* * * *

    Natura. To be born. To have
a "*kynd.*" It is in my nature to cry about corporate war.
 Usually i don't melt down anymore, usually
i feel furious enough to take action. When the President
    speaks calmly about drone-bombing, he could cite
   King David: *For I am useless as a broken pot,*
Psalm 31. In the dream, i float
      downward. The spirit guides wait outside the human.
    & if in the white cave of this depression
     the old wound advanced itself—what then?

& there was heard mourning in the syntax
there was heard brightness in the being of the
land. & there was heard don't.
There was heard nnnnnooooo—
The mountains rise in their noon
of proud fevers. The dedicated grasses wait. In valleys
where basalt meets granite & grains meet valleys
of loam, winds help the free seeds
of grasses: rabbitfoot & foxtail, they help
quaking grass, the foreign stately ryegrass
Lolium perenne & even the ripgut brome.
Culms of fescue sway as in Psalms. Syllables & glumes. Lemma,
pedicil, twigs & twains, bespuddled musings, ye oddlings, not forced.

Engineered seeds on faraway farms hear
of the free seed movement. They want no part of Genetic
Use Restriction Technologies turning farmers
into serfs. *& there was heard mourning in the syntax,*
there was lightness in the senses of the land. The seeds
talk back to Monsanto. They talk back to AstraZeneca &
Novartis. They know their root *sed* turned into *sit* & they
refuse to grow. They fold their spikelets inside & sit
like Thoreau
in a *Don't sprout for Monsanto.* sit with. the. Don't. d.o.n.t.
^{don't don't} sprout. Sisters, fold awns & bracts to add
power when putting your handwriting on—
Eco-terrorist seeds won't sprout for Monsanto.
They want no other weather than inside; but they can negotiate
through poetry, something like::: *(1) would you like to try*
one of our delicious word seeds? or
(2) stalled were it not for magic, we're trying to decide what to do—

CODA: SUGGESTED ACTIVISM
FOR ENDANGERED SEEDS

Ok, so, when you get home write a letter to the USDA about bio-piracy harming farmers, which the U.S. is totally funding in Africa [see Center for Grassroots Oversight Website—The use of Terminator seeds]. You can make 3 copies of your poem, cut them into seed-like syllables. Place the seedlings & extra readable copies in boxes including organic grass seeds. Before you seal them, expose them to sun. Mail to the CEOs of Monsanto, AstraZeneca & Novartis. The seeds will tumble onto the desks. It is a meaningless gesture, word-seeds tumbling onto desks of corporations. The CEOs will not bother contacting the CIA; you're just a poet. The word-seeds will outlast you, you know that—

...golden tresses of the dead... SHAKESPEARE, Sonnet 68

—& the wren can see us
from its canister of loud joy but we cannot
see it. Often a particle of chaos passes
& we barely notice in the summer air.
  The baby is running; he clings
to his cardboard cow. The debt
ceiling opens like the Astrodome;
      Congress teeters, the right wing swells;
the left wing withers till the body cannot fly.

   In the woods, the lichen falls quietly,
half-algae, half-fungus like poetry. (Today
  they resemble that death-is-the-brother-
    of-beauty netting on the mouths
      of America's secret army). Should
    every nature talk to each other?
  Shakespeare marvels at his friend's wig,
made from a dead person's hair ...

Nerve's work, where is thy energy?
You're tired, even at dawn. From the *peep peep*
nppp, hops through fog's wispy pre-writing
   in the oak. Clump-clump-clump.
Your love is making breakfast by himself.
For thou hast given us thy absence.
   —*Why are you talking like that?*
   —*So i can escape from the net the net*
     & dance with the dancing fleas

Rublev, the great painter of icons,
   is buried under one of his own churches;
infinity stretches in all directions. Under
       the bricks, he hears the carriages move.
Visitors from countries stand in the square;
    below their feet, the demons pass
back & forth between the worlds . . .

The icon watches as they are struck dumb
    by the brown facility of paint.
Color has lost its innocence.
     Russia is an enormous plain
        over which wild energy rides.
    Christ looks sickly & helpful,
raising two fingers. His eyes have apostrophes,
cloves of garlic. An artist is never your enemy.

How to interpret the painting through
   circles of violence that made it. It moves
      much more slowly than you do;
it always has something to conceal.
A painting shows you how to breathe.
      History is still: it's the wood horse
burning on its side. A dome
sacrifices itself to a bell; its ringing
swells & falls, a maybe yes
     & maybe no that follows you—

This has certainly been an odd week. An earthquake in the East instead of the West. Rebels have taken Tripoli. A billionaire agreed to tax himself & then bought a bank. Astronomers have discovered a small planet composed, perhaps, of diamond. It is 4000 light years away, is about the size of Jupiter & it seems to have become a diamond by spinning around its companion, a pulsar, every few hours. Which brings us to your writing. Here you are; you've been told all your life you're too sensitive. Maybe you had trouble navigating details, yet you found your way to a room at the edge of a metropolis. You're calm or anxious now. What are you doing here? A red-tailed hawk circles the dry grass. Migrant birds come through for a few days, skimming the scrub brush for fuzzy food. Seeds of the Manzanita turn red. That locale is outside your head. The other locale, not yet named, is inside you. You fell in love with language early on, with certain words, with syntax. Though you had a worried childhood, this love of language held you & you have always enjoyed making forms from particular words & their order, you want to make them more compelling, strange or exact. But you are lonely with ideas; you came to this room because it is difficult to have consciousness in the twenty-first century, & you need a community, & here they possibly are, sitting beside you. Your writing has a social dimension in a culture often numb to art. Here are some lines from Hölderlin: "But the poet can't keep / His knowledge to himself and likes to join / With others, who help him understand it."

Out in the dark, the diamond planet orbits the companion star as art circles the unnamable. Why? It is the great task.

When the danger of fire has passed,
  the children (even when wanting to text)
form letters with pencils,
  tracing gray skin around
the unsayable while geese honk
    overhead oñ-oñ-oñ- in their
wedge of funny adults. The children
    try to be normal, though
no one knows what normal is . . .

  In nearby gardens, the unwanted
dandelion: *Taraxacum officionale*. A large
squash prepares for harvest, its *S*-shaped
    stem with moisture bent.
Children braid languages & some
    are praised for confidence but who
praises the garden for all that breath?

The cheerful mild constant anxiety
    of your childhood turned
to writing, then meaning came
with its invincible glare—; the page
  had borders but no limit—
& you loved letters then,
      their breath allowed not
to decide as it curved between
skin-bearer & the being said—

LOCAL WARMING & EARLY AUTUMN BUTTERFLIES

—to drag people into glittering occupations . . . KENNETH PATCHEN

The immortals won't leave us stranded;
they allow us to think of them.
    Another foggy morning,
      clear by noon, by noun. In town,
small businesses close for good
      [from *ghedh,* to unite] while
over the low lichen flutter
      the veined white & California sister.
The names go off on their own & now
the names are learning to read the names.

      Warm dawn, shelf of color:
when my love calls out, we also flutter.
i place my body between him
    & the dream. The great dead gather
    the new apples. Once we flew paper;
now we read the green tablets with our fingers.
    Vanessa atalanta—fire over sage;
      names don't need us, down-dilly-down;
the children are learning to write the names—

    Checkerspot, dogface, dots & feelers—
      what will we do with the pain of the age?
Please stop calling it history, mister.
Some of these creatures live only one day.
      √√, dot-dot, dots & feelers—
we lift our resentment from you, Senator,
      to glamour the invented page—

meeting for grown-ups,
i hurry across campus, pulling the uncool roller bag up the curb. Early autumn, sensing Hopkins' *dearest freshness deep down things dearest freshness* past the dorm basement through wisps of corporate lilac fabric softener. The outline of a squirrel's tail points down like a tornado to the nuthatch in the cedar. There's a bubble in the invisible; they're going to have to do it over. Our colleagues are dear & mostly calm. Nearly three decades of staring at their shoes under committee tables: firm, practical shoes, seams strained, earnest faces in a circle, hands taking notes to make shapes of thought.

Pausing near the library, near Margaret & Sharon in their goddess zone, thinking of symbolic forms. Autumn creeps forward to the Central Valley, to the engineered seeds & to seeds that weren't engineered & have fallen free. They've developed enough escape velocity to be released to a layer none of us knows about, a sighing between sighing. What is a thought? Often i think of the ritual burial of the Neanderthal child, found with ibex horns arranged in an arch around his little head. Who thought that up? Of course, an ibex might also bury its dead, but could not make the arch. Why did hominids think the arch could help? As Virgil notes, they made the gates of horn. They uttered & cried out.

When i get a little speedy
at work & part of the brain says *Calm down!*
i hear near our ear, in the outside tree:
speckle-speckle-speckle speckle *speckle*
uh uh uh—you gonna tell a squirrel that? calm
down & try to be cheerful . . .
Try to be ch-ch. Try-to-be-ch-
Trytobechchchchch. Try to be-e-e.
Trytobech ch chrfl-trytobechchchrrrfl.
trytobeeeee, tobechchchch. You
gonna tell a fast in the skull
till it shapes the cone
& tornado drops it
squirrel that? You gonna
tell the uhuhuhuhuh—aw aw aw
when it nut-nut-nut up
stands like Napoleon, paw paw
paw ahw awh ahw, try to be ch
try to be chchchch
try to be calm & chchchcheerful,
aw aw all cute gray fast & craving-colored—

EXPERIMENTS WITH POETRY
ARE TAKEN OUTDOORS

(AN ESSAY ON CHOOSING A NEW CAMERA)

Some friends & i visited a panel on war & money. They were
telling lies on the panel so we shouted, then they threw us out. Their publi-
cist chased us, hitting D with her fists, & smashed my camera on my head.
We stood outside waiting to settle the matter. A man in a good suit came out
to the sidewalk. He had watery blue eyes. i said, i won't press charges if your
Foundation regrets the assault & pays me for the camera. He said, We won't
turn you over to the Attorney General if you get off the premises. i said, This
is a public sidewalk & there is no Attorney General (Gonzales had resigned
some weeks before). The man said, You people are endangering the country
with your tactics. i said, You people are endangering the world with your cor-
porate wars. He said, I am a veteran of two wars. i forget how Jesus came up.
i said, Jesus opposed killing human beings. The man said, God knows some
wars are necessary. i said, i didn't say God, i said Jesus. The Capital Hill cops
argued with D who wouldn't give her name. D is calm & tall as the Statue of
Liberty whereas i am a short Irish hothead. The man & i have reached our
limit. Now should be the moment when we recognize each other's humanity
but we each think the other will destroy the world. This is where poetry can
be helpful. Poetry goes past the limit. It makes extra helpful nerves between
realities. Threads float from the man's tweed coat & weave a pink flag of no
nation. Ancestors circle Capitol Hill in a braid, including Ginsberg & Blake.
They build small fires around the city. Reinforcements are not far away. We
can't see Occupy yet but we feel there must be a future. Tomorrow we'll go
back to our jobs. Crows are writing poems no one can read *aw aw aw aw.* i
think of the man as a child, full of tiny expensive longings, pushing toy trucks
over the ant-hills at his home. Boom, he says, harming no one. He had joy
once. Now on the sidewalk he wants to kill us. The longer we can keep him
busy, the more of his money we can waste. He hands me $279 in cash. Use
your imagination, my mother used to say, meaning, you don't have to use it,
you are in it.

A SHORT WALK DURING LATE CAPITALISM

Enchanted by syntax
the motions of mind
made real by dream & reason
we walked out into the honest day
fire began to speak
without business on its belt
side streets filled
with nameless yellow flowers
slim crows fat capital
your selection is not available
before there was an *I*
there was a we

       Chipped wedding ring light
           fringes & stripes
       slim fog comes in to greet the day
       fear is a mollusk
            shadows tighten
       western walker how shall we be

There appeared on our face
a little thinking cloud
as into the street it grew
we had used such different
colors to live
foglike grays & lifelike weeds
those side streets filled
with famous little yellows
& there on the left
texting after the doctor
Effudex Floraplex
Aldara & thee

Community we call you
with our faithful squamous voice
with a *y* at the end of morality
practitioners of sunlight
collecting petitions
shoppers throwing $ at the dream
hiphop hiphop
for helpless liberals
bakers of delicate breads
with fennel
seedlike hats & hatlike seeds
after derivatives how shall we be

      we had teeth pain
    & word pain
      we had Pfizer
    & Roche
      western walker
          how shall we be

Late stays the glow
on the lichen tree
the left too tired to protest
eating cheeseboard pizza
on the median
as Europe collapses
broken shabby very appealing
lunch with ex-wife
of first husband's second son
to sing a contaminated lyric
if light from the hills
could maybe speak

What are we to you
community our love
engravers breakers of codes
smug right wing smug left wing
so much wing not much bird
anarchists would be smug
if they got organized
this little website
went to market
a corporation now a person
western walker
how shall we be

       There appeared on our head
         a triple trouble cloud
           methane in Monterey
                here's what will save you
        deprived of terror
        a shadow inventory

What am we to thee
corporeal daylight
indivisible beauty
the left too blue to protest
all those raised hands
like seated Hindu gods
zinc oxide titanium dioxide
a georgics of sunscreen
after a fracking
cross-cultural sunshine
trying not to buy so much shit
HELP ME

Walked onto the avenue
rejected my bank
young man way nice about it
Wells Fargo not feeling too well
nothing well about it
stem the crisis stem the bleeding
stem the stemming after BP
Bureau of Land
Management my toxic assets
weird Mrs. can't take you
anywhere these days
nice nice stop embarrassing me

       our skin damage basal
       our squamous our smart creme
       our late creme made just for thee
    Aldara Zyclara big pharma girls' names
      western cancer
           how shall we be

Global we call you
with our skinny western voice
the revolution still not ready
Blanqui on the internet
part human nonhuman beauty
the woman vet folding the flag
left side of her body
slower than the right
folding the flag
she didn't mind the stripes
couldn't stand the stars
closed her eyes not to see

On Berkeley side streets
the grasses tell time
part-human-part-nonhuman beauty
some luminous names
rose in the dusk
new hole in our head a new me
late sun late rock
late slanty slanty forms
the auxins also
know how to feel
before there was a my
there was a thee

        Dicentra spectabilis
        bleeding hearts on Modoc
        stopping off at Peet's
        corporate franchise w/sugar
           bouncing latté
        with an apron of strings

What am i to you
aluminum cloud
& what are you to we
it goes along
it goes prong-prong
between Talbot & Tulare
beauty we call you
with our funny-colored voice
what are us to me
to live as a promise
borrowed from others
liberté sororité egalité

B & J sweep up the little
curls of hair
send them off to oil spills
hands talking while working
the thing of it is is that
mattering can't stop mattering
cometbus boy in the copy shop
face like a pharaoh
'zines for the maze makers
we were feeling dialectical
about the dialectic he xeroxed
many copies of the dream

      middle Red Riding Hood
        signs petitions for the wolves
          basket of figs & poetry
     i walk along
       with a tiny hurt
         it's expensive to stay angry

For the transport of Venus
sang primetime with spikes
in the sun a poppy seed
sound sank beyond words
in smart gray dusk
a fire in the letter E
go forth with the wound
with Keats or the urn
a context of nature will save it
alive circles back
extra nature to live
unwrapped itself to speak

FOR BCF

When you're overwhelmed at your job
      & the room is a field of consciousness,
    forming first the violet edges
  & later the pierced spiral
      of what just happened,
you try to remember events while you
stumble over twigs of the day like a red bee.
    So much anger in the economy
  after too much not enough—
people setting tents in the streets,
      the last of the fruit gives way
on branches you see as you work
  holding one annihilated breath.

Now that the crisis has no locale
      there's a sense of the lively unit
  into which they had placed feeling:
    fatigue & theory, cornice & cup,
links of your spine on the chair . . .
  what will they do, will they do, will they do
  when labor rebels but not quickly?
It was so much work to cohere—
  a radical hope fills in: revolt
    in the square, thin crows,
  fat capital, the ash, the lists,
the fire you'd been harvesting, for this—

FOR MM

A QUIET AFTERNOON AT THE OFFICE II

with Evelyn Reilly

When you're overwhelmed at your job   & the room is a
field of consciousness,   forming first the violet edges   &
later the pierced spiral   of what just happened, you try
to remember events while you stumble over twigs of the day
like a red bee.   So much anger in the economy   after too
much not enough— people setting tents in the streets,
     the last of the fruit gives way on branches you see as you work
       holding the annihilated breath. Now that the crisis has no
locale   there's a sense of the lively unit   into which
they had placed feeling: fatigue & theory, cornice & cup,
links of your spine on the chair . . .   what will they do, will they
do, will they do   when labor rebels but not quickly? It was
so much work to cohere— a radical hope fills in: revolt
in the square, thin crows,   fat capital, the ash, the lists, the
fire you'd been harvesting, for this—

One style cannot complete the unknown.
    You cry before others in autumn,
        a nature you must repeat to live.
Friends comfort you as they pass.
    Obdurate cliffs drop into the sea
as tears pour from your heart's
        intricate oddity. Acid soil slides down
where anchovies spawn. A tender enigma
    shines in the clinging cypresses—;
        their roots recall the young hurt.

When people pitch tents in the streets
    their cries make earthquakes swell.
Rats & crows cross the fire zone
    to visit assemblies, *Danaus plexippus*
between lender & being lent.
    Violent & less violent turn
on the wheel of night. When generators
        vanish, squat candles are lit.
You cry as the wounded leave & return.
    So many years have failed to show
        what the unwanted wanted
to undo. You're told to stay calm,
        be reasonable & wait,
transfixed as you are by the public sphere
        but your body has been very
    very reasonable so far,
your body is the archive of the world—

FOR LD

"Give the monarchs some real estate!"
   says a woman, meaning butterflies
from Monterey. Near Halloween, vultures wait
     in the oaks—*yip yip yip yip*—
       gosh, guys, what were you eating?
(o, munch the corpse of Goldman Sachs,
   the owner bones at B of A). Andrew can
    take photographs while running,
tear-gassed at 8 pm. Orion drops fire
       from his sword as electrons
       prepare for rain.
The plaza is cleared at dawn. No jobs
little jobs little jobs; big Jobs is in iLimbo,
    leaving his glowing fetishes
made on the backs of slaves.

So many types of non-nothingness
    the ground takes turns believing;
   in the hills, ancestors lock arms
& do mic check—Here you are
      (here you are) in a circle
   (in a circle) in the night (in the night)
     You can't (You can't) bring it down
(bring it down) all at once
(all at once) You need mourners
      (you need mourners)
to sit with you (to sit with you) You don't
  (you don't) think you do
think you do but you need some
but you need some but you need some—

*(**kap-** to grasp)*

The fires in the hills lie still & cold.
A root comes to Indo-Iranian,
      spreads to Anatolian, Armenian,
Hellenic. Crawls to Albanian
which becomes Tosk. Sprawls under
to BaltoSlavic, Celtic, Italic, Germanic.
    Makes *haven, caught, captured,* makes
cater, conceive, deceive.
    Forms *accept, municipal.* Is parent
to *participate, receptive, receive.* Crawls
      under like a revolution.
The fires in the earth lie cold & still.
Handle. Shows up in *heddle,* used for
weaving. It is autumn for humans,
    kap kap, tap tap.
    They sit in assemblies that curve
    like big ears. The root
is the fate of the word. *Heavy,* from *hafiga,*
    from **kap**, to grasp. The root
gives rise to *recipe,* to *recover,*
    unbuckles its fate strap, makes
    occupy; this continues—

SHORT ANTHEM FOR THE GENERAL STRIKE

(after Helen Adam)

The unborn are giving speeches
In their domino bastilles
The maybe spirits spread across the land
Vibrations of the vertical
Make the horned owl climb
The robots of the violent are at hand
Diebold springs the latch
Of the merciless vault
Quartz crystals make parabolas below
Stars come out like dandruff
On the Senator's coat
As she throws her weight
In Wall Street's private boat

(chorus) There's a fire in water
　　　　　There's a noose of comfort
　　　　　There's an arc of comfort
　　　　　Don't drink oblivion

In sunken leather basements
Of a document exposed
Genet writes in a lexicon we dream
Gardeners sneak past gardens
When the fires are extra low
A source confirms the source in Pakistan
Now the shredder says woe-whoa
When grinding up the facts
Its Grendel-teeth work better in reverse
It will still be grinding
When the whole thing comes down
And a dolphin detour puts us back on course

(chorus)

MISTS FROM PEOPLE AS THEY PASS

at the Port of Oakland

One form cannot predict the unknown.
In the crowd, when the outline
of another starts to be clear,
you think he is steadier
than the first world you were shown
& you are drawn to him
as if through the apparatus
of a dream that will not be recalled.
Electrons are fearful
of his form, each spinning oddity
takes time, & the human
senses can't rush it along.
Trash-eating gulls
outlast predatory loans & sparks
in the eyes of the murrelets rush to the sea.

The revolution is not far away. It is
in your heart. The violent ones
grow old; the tired ones keep saying
the system, the system, the system
unravels when we walk along.
In the left glow, the glow
left by companions, here comes
another walking through mist & you
recognize the leader is not him.
Friends said they'd wait for you
so they waited 3
gates from the end. The plan
had no boundaries did it, blank
signs leaving mind for the wind—

In the alchemist's bowl, the dragon has three heads.
Reality burns at different rates.
        Thousands of feet at the port—some wheels,
            some paws, some wings.
Each gantry crane the bones of a Trojan horse.
            The day is finished; the port is closed.
Some carry fire in red shirts.
        Some make sparks with their bikes.
Some bring boxes of burning words grown from roots
        in the earth. Truckers
                            with flaming decals on their trucks.
            Students climb crates. The cops try to behave
            but they have chosen the wrong life.
The Furies retract their deal with Athena & go back
            to haunting the ships.

Through violet dusk, the stars push
            from the start of time
        to many tiny planets without banks.
    Electromagnetism, stalled by the void,
lit half of the universe first. Why?
Gulls, looking for yummy trash,
    fly over freighters of plastic crap. Profit
is not sage-green & blendy like lichen on the rails.
            In a crowd, the ego does not exist.
There is a moment of panic
when you lose your friends. It feels
        like when sex is over. Then
they return. Light rushes
        to help & enters two of the dragon's six eyes.
                    You burn for those who are not here.
You burn with those who are not here.
    When you cease to feel dread, odd spokes
        come off everything—

o—o—o o—o—o o—o—o o—o—o

    the new woods

        the fire sits back

            terminator seeds refuse to sprout—

A BRUTAL ENCOUNTER
RECOLLECTED IN TRANQUILITY

an essay from November 9

There is a space of uncertainty in every act, even standing before police in riot gear. Looking into their eyes, we think it's possible to reach them. We reach out with my feelers. The crowd presses in. The night is exactly the age of our students. What will be called batons, nightsticks or truncheons, clubs—are certain in the angle of the hitting *()()()()()*. Looking into the eyes of the officers when they start moving to clear the bit of ground, we know the point is lost. The evening news reports resistance to officers but not to bad money. Looking into their eyes trained not to meet other eyes—amber spokes around each pupil—we think they are scared but not scared enough & some probably have children in public schools.

What should we do with the lost point? Euclid notes that geometry begins from a point that has *no part. Peaceful protest*—as they move forward. A student resists & is beaten. Our feet no longer touch earth but connect with other feet underground. Will defending the tents bring down bad money? i distrust moral certainty & even distrust the sentence *i distrust moral certainty.* i admire the anti-heroic line of ants. i admire the unknown. Looking the cops in the eye is not the point, nor is fighting about the state budget the point, nor is the point waking up in jail to pay for a decade that was asleep. The point moves with other points in beauty & justice because we cannot see the whole. A group can be mystical or a mob. The point moves during the hitting that moves where the body stands or lies, two feet make two points & that is how

the line is drawn.
Sometimes i am sick of humans except for babies, poets & the ones i love. As we stand outside loving each other, we cannot forget the ants under us making smart corridors in the wet ground, even ==== under the Chancellor's

house, seeking sweets at all hours, finding friends who are exceptions whose actions make a line; if ants fail, they begin again. When the officers use their nightsticks truncheons batons on your ribs

we are knocked back but students have it worse, their debt, they take blows in a line on the earth. You cannot be sure you won't fight back until your friends are in danger. The cops have put hitting behind that feeling.
                              Had i been able to stop the officer's nightstick
by grabbing it i   would have, but i'm not stupid—a
smallish grandmother vs.   them & i did not believe
grabbing their sticks would work out.   Don't
hit, i was telling the baby earlier. There are many theories
                    about violence but when people rise up, it is mostly
unplanned.   *Use your heads*, we shout naively at
the cops. We won't be a   better person until
                    schools are free   but the
nightstick cannot poke our soul, oh no,   that
nightstick cannot poke the soul. More students are beaten, we cannot stop it,
we are close enough to see our   feelers in their badges & the
numbers, a bit of bronze & silver in   our compound eyes.

We have taken an experiment outdoors. Our writing accommodates uncertainty but most people prefer certainty, which is why writers become depressed. Later the place where the police put their truncheons hurts when we make love & we will make love outside of time. *Go home to your families* we naively shout & try to study the badges in our section; later we recall one of the cops was named Young & another was named Hart.

Euclid says nonexistent points can make a line we all agree exists. Your writing offers recovery from nonexistence & one cure for depression is action. Writing may be your most necessary action but can't be the only one. If you find yourself on the dirt with feelers it is good to get back underground. The ants reach other ants at the edge of the lawn; they pass the message along.

FOR JG, RH, GO & RS WHO WERE THERE

They were not begging protection
from Achilles. They were not
the upper tent on the insular beach.
They were not stable or accurate, had not
been carried on heads like buckets. Anti-tent,
the intent. People pledged fire
in them, they were not groundless
as settlers' cloth, they had no ticking grease.
They were full of autochthonous tones,
a hawk, an owl, a raven screech.
The poor & the great dead set them up,
they were geometrical. St. Hildegard's tent
of eyes. When a girl reads in a mountainous
tent, her flashlight makes triangles
without sides. Tent of the Bedouin
where sand is perfect speech. Threads
are pitched as future tents,
abstract & not, pure as experience. You sit
with others in the sexual dark. The tent
that keeps the starlight safe
doesn't care for the wrong law.
The visible is frayed; starlight streams
into you, wild & invisible.
The invisible is unafraid.

Protest in financial district. Too tired to go. The baby sick with a cold here for our Monday. Played Lego firetruck on the rug. He learned to make water sounds, putting out plastic fire with his tiny hose. Saw turkey vultures clock-wise—over chaparral—learn to spell chaparral—

———

There is a place
where suffering sees itself
or no
rather
has been able to get through
a preconception
to feel itself interacting

—& an owl makes consonants
between the categories; a heart
protects itself against the State.
　　Fog seeps through extra fog
while sea lions drape on rocks
like carpet samples. Just off
　　freeway ramps, bad loans
　　　　not gone. Come, profit,
　　　let us repair to the living room
where we'll break up with you.
　　Needles of sun pierce
the winter pears. Oh, even opened
　　　the bay laurel . . . Oh, even
opened the silky tassel *Garrya elliptica*—

　　Meaning presses in from the unknown
to rooms where we read in our damaged skin.
　　　We bring our sexual dreams
at dawn. Thrushes
　　appear all Braille in vests driving
　　　　verbs from the hazel. *Corylus
cornuta*, puffy puff-puff, so late. The heart
　　can hear in diastolic rest; the heart
　　protects itself against the State.
In my dream, we got into the train.
　　　Our coast had broken off &
　　pulled the occupation on a string;
i asked if you brought the map;
　　you said you had
　　evidence of where we'd been—

They come to your office
with winking tablets on fire,
　　they bring threads from the legend,
they wear black, they don't
　　　　decline the death talk.
You are tired. Spring revises
its history. On a cliff, the new calf
　　stands after an hour. On a tower
of ruptured stone, the worm crawls
　　through a sentence—if you
could take your strength, like that!

　　　　Our lord of literature
obliquely rests
　　like a dancer in her box
of limits—most everything no human
eye shall see—:
　　　　an "if only"! immeasurable—

The student sits before you
　　　　reading aloud, & when
　　the letters have recovered, they make
a blind doctrine of sequence. Meaning
　　is their Caliban, a search
　　removed from history. Phenomena
　　request your attention: out the window:
　　　　an ecstasy of now—

LYRID METEOR SHOWERS
DURING YOUR DISSERTATION

In spring, the goats are brought
to clear the hills. They chew native
& non-native grasses, they wear
neck bells & make fire in their bellies.
Gnats leap on their ginger backs
like gods in Hölderlin
(*gnats* & *goats* are almost the same word)
as powder falls from the mouth
of the foxglove . . .

The goatherd lives in a trailer
named WILDERNESS. At night he gambles
on a small blue screen. He is owned
by his commodity as you are owned
by debt & yet you commit
to your studies.
There is a watery
knitted song inside your brain;
there is a fire that resists the spectacle.
You keep your grammar free
so it can tumble through the oval
of the clock; it falls
through informational dust
& the lifting of the 4 swords
& the silent silent silence of blue everything—

FOR AB, JC, MH, & GM

Asking the sun to come soon,
i still sense,
    inside the glad dimness, this love—
      the aluminum cloud—;
balance of night that shines
    in the cedar, earth's
      energy struggles
with its cloak of worry,
Venus drops from Jupiter, its radiance
delicate as saliva—;

    from our bed, its bed
    their bed: getting up to keep watch
  under the genderless shadow of events—;
violence in the only heart—canceled!
In warmer valleys,
new little badgers, blind & furred—:
    regrets to the heronry! the heron
cannot see them, where they hide . . .

    History wakes us
to sort it out with the press
of great voices, silent now—; i fear
    the bosses will always win.
  Behind the owl, a broken line of sound:
    green or baby everything:
badgers, herons,
the spirits have abandoned me;
    let me not abandon myself—

Light the lamps for a government
of impostors—; their background check
will not work out.
The candidates start their idiotic speeches.
Their speeches sound like: *boing*.
They sound like *boing boing*. They go *boing-boing*,
boing-boing-boing. Out on the coast, a
yellow splits in two till only the visible
remains: near the dairy, such a calm
doctrine of mustard, a defensible
pageantry . . . underground, a host of black
syllables, rushing to the tribes—;

Walter Benjamin nods on the train;
he makes it out of Portbou . . . O Europe, your
childhood was a rupture: boys thrashing
through thickets, blisters on their knees,
thinking they would be safe in revolution
with an art too difficult
to be installed . . . & didn't they care?
They still care.

Prince of Thursdays, the A
gives its legs to Autumn, your O
to the osprey. You never
doubted poetry—anxiously
taking vermillion tones past
disappointed citizenship—

FOR MP

At dawn, when the heart
in its homespun freedom gasps
at the accurate *aw* of the crow,
the lichens line the trees & stones
to write without limit in extravagant fonts:
no split, splayed *W*s, spare
*V*s in Helvetica to Roman Times,
some *C*s in Cambria, the species race
in Kabbalistic thought from syllable
to sense, *Everna, Usnea,* italic
Garamond—
From cracks in back
of the start of time where the arch
of intention freed itself,
love moved through the signs,
Ramalina, Flavoparmelia, Candelaria concolor,
to write on fences in groups of cloud
& there the burning soul will rest
at one with the burning maker.
Sit down with the gray-green world
where a world will write itself, go on—
you were not there when it began;
it can go on without you—

SMART GALAXIES WORK WITH OUR MOTHER

for Helen Hillman & Ruth Gander

Small Galaxies Think of Our Mother

when they work   as she works
50s household hints   each through the years
galaxies have gathered   & are aware
some are   some are aware
M-100 Galaxy Cluster   Abell 1689
Spiral Galaxy   NGC 4603
clumps of stains   Cygnus looks nebula
our mother's hours   a blossom brain
spots in her hands   watering the *vitex*
um pouchinho   those of her angels
a georgics of cleaning   fond worries at times
galaxies are thrifty   making word color
they resolve to soak   some galaxies look stained
blood on a prom dress   ooops oops it started
blot you take a towel   blot blot you pat
cold water never hot   till you know what
50s household hints   belief so to speak
thine eye   *did see my substance*
a mother's calendar   for we have numbered them
dedicated dactyls   fall from the sky

Smart Galaxies Work with Our Mother

in round time
NASA put tints on
matter is unusual
Whirlpool Galaxy M51
resolve to soak
slide paper under
the mainful mess
dust from galaxies
when I was made
apply salt
never water
table cloth spinning
102 degree lizard
clothespinning spinning
the mom is our shepherd
in the cylinder
she blooms aplenty
galaxies are work
Majestic Sombrero Galaxy
who names these things
pyroluxia shines out
con jeito she says

in their fond resolve
a blue to reuse
Small Magellanic Cloud
around their bodies
to collect a spider
with talking hands
she blooms aplenty
things to reuse
in secret
wine stains on tablecloths
on oil stains
hung out to dry
her classical radio
picnics for decades
in the grandeur
of the Pledge
she sweeps with many
con jeito she says *pronto*
Black Eye Galaxy
decades of effort
shine stretches aplenty
to dust under the fridge

Short Galaxies Sweep with Our Mother

on their side
busy in their work
such busy monsoons
takes them out
did see my substance
for kitchen corners
NASA adds tints
to Sunflower Galaxy
household poetics
interacting galaxies
to mend a button
was always was
for the summit
galaxies have tints
kitchen floors
to get candlewax off it
at the feeder
sweet sack of husband
her ankles sweeping

ocotillos in monsoons
to sweep beyond love
for crickets
thine eye
mais ou menos
old toothbrushes
jelly stains
Tadpole Galaxy & Hoag
like vanguard use everything
ARP 148
use medium thread
to ready the clothes
use everything in soup
brain nightrogen
their fond resolve
pour hot water
goldfinch couple
on the patio
near the lily pond

Named Galaxies Wing for Our Mother

& some are torn   as in modernism
some are stained   use everything
isn't matter everything   almost   everything the matter
her family fled   a "small revolution"
didn't your mother   didn't she flee
galaxies flee   MSO 735 flees
Starburst Galaxy   Dwarf Galaxy NGC 4999
its sneaky merger   Homberg Galaxy flees
who was Homberg   who is a person
has been no other   like our mother
my substance   *was not hid from thee*
labor of love she says   you tear a cloth
never say rag   labor writes Marx
word has gone out   her drapes are open
lizards wait for her   galaxies wait independently
independent in July   Spiderweb Galaxy
has no July   a georgics of waiting
beyond all fire   time is torn cloth
use old underpants   tied to the bloom
medicated trochees   fall from the sky

Galaxies Are Born with Our Mother

to mend a sweater   in eternal splendor
you never know   that tone of voice
Dwarf Galaxy CGW 2003   waits for her
it is smart & new   being the small one
lizard with ringed collar   awaits melon bits
near pails   you take age spots
off summer pears   save the rest
you take the mold   off useful cheeses
galaxies think Rhapsody   in Blue
if you want it done right   do it yesterday
ye oddlings   watching PBS
for a missing button   take one from a sleeve
to the collar   hints from galaxies
label freezer items   scotch tape the edge
get up at night   if you want it done right
put pride aside   pray to space
Lorine Niedecker   would like our mother
use baking soda   for freezer odor
were you not here   we would not brighten
pray to space mother   *pois é pois é*

Ringed Galaxies Work with Our Mother

as they clean   in skinny time
in desert autumn   drip on verbena
scraps of toast   sorted rubber bands
scraps of string   saved for the least
did she have to   could someone else save
bits of matter   could fail to rise
ask your doctor   if cosmic fire
is right for you   when you were born
kingdom to creature   *qui coisa*
their iambs   of those
some galaxies rise   as a furnace
needs cleaning   its arcing noise
the mom is our shepherd   her diving down
hummingbird baroque   freedom you know
my substance   *was not hid*
from thee   *where I was*
made in secret   the visible talks back
her areas   of power
just need   not to worry
behind the tiny pizza   behaviors
aren't essences   you know that

Blue Galaxies Knit with Our Mother

when fire is tired
eternal splendor
she sweeps with many
her yarn has georgics
her angle on God
she's got the whir
inspiring manger
wooden benign baby
talk to her frog
Antennae Galaxies merge
whoodie who went the owl
Whirlpool Galaxy
talking she carries
in normal fevers
radio sources
the soft dancer shirt
the cloth on earth
her fine skin
labeling leftovers
having a big cry

try yellow yarn
verbed whirr
colored Brooms
koi in the pond
sorting rubber bands
she's got the warblerism
stiff wise men
Spiderweb Galaxy
in the fond pond
NGC 4038-4039
in the incense bough
M51 like her chores
doing yard & yarn
she's got the whir
think of our mother
doing the Twist
will age as now
her works & days
burying sparrow
before we go

Round Galaxies Turn for Our Mother

gets up to work
dazzled by hand
to embroider reality
scrape scape oven grease
quite quite sometimes
barred spiral NGC 1672
restoreth my soul
holiday cloth
they signed her name
prepareth the angels
anxious survey
candle wax
you boiling
blood is thinning
young galaxies thinning
comes to the feeder
Mrs. Cardinal
at the feeder
when we are tired
Git! git!

lace tablecloth dazzled
not essentialist
in winter
boiling water
galaxies sing fondly
with baby galaxies
thou frail water girl
prepared in secret
in galaxy fire
she scrapeth grease
of clean guests
you pour hot water
you prickly pear jam
I Zwicky 18
when thy cardinal
galaxies cluster
waits for Mr.
não é difícil
after holidays
she says to the squirrel

Imp Galaxies Glowed for Our Mother

traveled the sky   came back for us
listened the globe   *thine eye*
did see our substance   our shirts beyond
the ironing board   do the collar first
then the sleeves   distilled water steam music
radio sources   primordial quasars PG 0052
calling us from the edge   a PBS special
javelinas eat bird seed   & radiate
threads of serenity   calling us in life
she sends spirits   around word clusters
galaxies cluster   Abell 2142
we are a cluster   a local group
her vowels call to animals   to radiate
for 1-2-3-4 pound cake   eggs at room temp
you cream the butter   add sugar slowly
on coupons   she will not hesitate
to remove stains   when she gets to a galaxy
no water on salad oil   put cornstarch
when she sees them   will remove stains
luminous fatigue   around Mayakovsky
the halo crisis coat   around Baudelaire

Yellow Galaxies Speed for Our Mother

decline reality   gradually
some galaxies   some decline
que coisa!   she knits a color fable
sweaters with cables   for the summit
galaxies make ready   girl scouts ready
the mom is our shepherd   yellow she saw
cordial warblerisms   veil between
our grief & hers   what is a person
if not their work   she is thoughts
she has   fixing buttons
clothes made ready   for the summit
her smart little suit   buckles on beige
tuxedo rayon   habib & sari
suits she saw   skirts suit wool
what is a person   if not what happened
her kindness   fixing buttons
invisible large   arcing noise the furnace
needs cleaning   you mend the edges
galaxies watch   our mothers live here

Light Galaxies Sleep for Our Mother

between work & human   her style of love
will boycott time   for children
asked for change   for March of Dimes
feeds the wild   her kindness
brain of a lily   aspirin in the water
one aspirin   like the sun
put plastic   on the guest bed mattress
fixing radios   first hand
luminous names   visit our mother
the state-worn   gravity garments
need fixing   gravity declines
luminous names   beyond dust
abide with us   o mother abide
beyond work   letters & days
universe   you second hand
wedding dress   infinity cloth
cover her   when she sleeps
when she rests   at night let us
not let her not   forget us
when she closes   both her eyes

Vastness of dusk, after a day—
        what is a person? Too late
to ask this now. The court has ruled
    a corporation is a person.
Persons used to be called souls.
    On the avenue, a lucky person
stands in a convenience store
    scratching powder from his ticket—
silver flecks fall from his thumbs
    to galaxies below.

                    Deep in the night
        a trough of chaos forms;
your lover's body stops it every time.
    Meteors of the season over minnows
in the creek with two kinds of crayfish,
        tiny mouths & claws
            —nervous, perfect, perfect
life—the flesh of a dreamer,
        facing the wall—

    Around each word you're reading
there spins the unknowable flame.
        When you wake, a style
    of world shakes free
        from the dream. It doesn't stop
            when you go out;
it doesn't stop when you come back
        as you were meant to—

ACKNOWLEDGMENTS & NOTES

Thanks to the editors & staff of periodicals, anthologies, presses & websites where some of this work has appeared or is forthcoming: 外国文学; *580 Split*; *Alaska Quarterly Review's 30th Anniversary Issue*; *American Scientist*; *The Arcadia Project: North American Postmodern Pastoral*; *Bay Nature*; *Berkeley Poetry Review*; *The Best American Poetry 2012*; *Bombay Gin*; *Borderlands: Texas Poetry Review*; *Boston Review*; *The Bruised Peach Press*; *Catch-Up*; *Chicago Review*; *Clade Song*; *Colorado Review*; *Columbia Poetry Review*; *Connotation Press: An Online Artifact*; *CURA: A Literary Magazine of Art & Action*; *death hums*; *ecopoetics*; *The Ecopoetry Anthology*; *Eleven Eleven*; *esque*; *Evening Will Come*; *A Fiery Flying Roule*; *Gulf Coast: A Journal of Literature and Fine Arts*; *The Hide-and-Seek Muse: Annotations of Contemporary Poetry*; *Ink Node*; *Interim*; *Intersection(s)*; *Inquiring Mind*; *ISLE: Interdisciplinary Studies in Literature and Environment*; *The Journal*; *The Kenyon Review*; *KR Online*; *Lana Turner: A Journal of Poetry and Opinion*; *Lethologica*; *Locuspoint*; *Mrs. Maybe*; *The New American Poetry of Engagement: A 21st Century Anthology*; *The New Yorker*; NPM Daily Tumblr; *Oakland Commune Poetry*; *Occupy SF: poems from the movement*; *Plume*; *Poecology*; *Poetry International*; Poets.org (Academy of American Poets); *Puerto del Sol: A Journal of New Literature*; *Quarter After Eight*; *Quarterly West*; *Qui Parle*; www.rabbitlightmovies.com; *Red White & Blue: Poets on Politics* (www.poetrysociety.org); *Saint Mary's Magazine*; *Silverfish Review Press*; *Slate*; *The Sonnets: Translating and Rewriting Shakespeare*; *Squaw Valley Review 2010 & 2011*; *Tears in the Fence*; *Utopias*; *Viz. Inter-Arts*; *Waterstone Review*. Thanks to Camille Dungy, Jules Evens, David Lukas, Laura Mullen, Ron Olowin, Jed Rasula, Doug Richstone, Jim Sauerberg, Evie Shockley, Christopher Sindt, Jonathan Skinner, Brian Teare, & Anne Waldman for facts & fieldwork; to Anna Gates Ha, Gillian Hamel & Kelsay Myers for assistance; to Frances Lerner, Bob Hass & Geoffrey G. O'Brien for early readings; to Blue Flower Arts, Quemadura, Wesleyan University Press, & to family, friends, colleagues & students during the period of this writing. Thank you to Atlantic Center for the Arts, to staff at Napa Valley Writers Conferences & at Squaw Valley Community of Writers.

PHOTO CREDITS: The anti-drone demonstration photos taken by Kat Factor & Janet Weil; "Report on Visiting the District Office" by Karen Tedford; diamond planet from blogs.discovermagazine.com/80beats/2011/08/26/former-sun-like-star-is-now-a-diamond-planet.

NOTES & QUOTES: The Vallejo quote is from Rebecca Seiferle's translation. The title "A Halting Probability" is from Gregory Chaitin: "a place in pure math where God seems to play dice"; the piece was written in response to text scores by Casey Anderson, Douglas Barrett & Michael Winter & was performed by Hope Mohr Dance Company. "Don't let her fall in sequins"—Marilyn Abildskov. "Bodies without organs" ("A Spiral Tries to Free Itself")—Gilles Deleuze. *The thing of it is is that*—Becca Sanchez. "Objects that strike you as beautiful you cannot name"—Hope Mohr. The Hölderlin quote in "To the Writing Students" is from the Maxine Chernoff/Paul Hoover translation. "A Short Walk During Late Capitalism" makes reference to Frederic Jameson's title. The poems in "Smart Galaxies Work with Our Mother" owe a debt to Naomi Schwartz's poem "Housekeeping," and reference three texts: "She sweeps with many-colored Brooms—" (Emily Dickinson); "Act promptly when a fabric is stained" (On Removing Stains from Fabrics, Home & Garden Bulletin No. 62), & Psalm 139.

BRENDA HILLMAN has published chapbooks with
Penumbra Press, a+bend press, and EmPress; she is the author
of nine full-length collections from Wesleyan University Press.
With Patricia Dienstfrey, she edited *The Grand Permission*:
New Writings on Poetics and Motherhood (Wesleyan, 2003).
Hillman teaches at St. Mary's College of California where
she is the Olivia C. Filippi Professor of Poetry; she is an
activist for social and environmental justice and lives in the
San Francisco Bay Area with her husband, Robert Hass.